BAKING
BIBLE

October 2010
To Janice
With much Love!
xxoox
Sally

BAKING
BIBLE
FROM THE OVEN TO THE TABLE

I still think About the
first time We Put
chocolate chips in
Warm Rice Krispies.
The Kids almost
didn't act any. :)

First published in 2009
Love Food ® is an imprint of Parragon Books Ltd

Parragon
Queen Street House
4 Queen Street
Bath BA1 1HE, UK

ISBN: 978-1-4075-6747-1

Printed in China

Additional photography by Clive Bozzard-Hill (pages: 49, 50, 57, 62, 85, 94,
103, 105, 109, 123, 127, 133, 134, 141, 165, 166, 171, 177, 178, 203, 207,
210, 216, 219, 221)
Additional food styling by Valerie Barrett (pages: 49, 50, 57, 62, 85, 94, 103,
105, 109, 123, 127, 133, 134, 141, 165, 166, 171, 177, 178, 203, 207, 210,
216, 219, 221)
Additional recipes written by Angela Drake (pages: 48, 56, 84, 104, 126,
132, 170, 176, 206, 211)

Notes for the Reader
This book uses imperial, metric, and US cup measurements. Follow the
same units of measurement throughout; do not mix imperial and metric.
All spoon measurements are level: teaspoons are assumed to be 5 ml, and
tablespoons are assumed to be 15 ml. Unless otherwise stated, milk is
assumed to be whole, eggs and individual vegetables, such as potatoes,
are medium, and pepper is freshly ground black pepper.

The times given are an approximate guide only. Preparation times differ
according to the techniques used by different people and the cooking
times may also vary from those given as a result of the type of oven used.
Optional ingredients, variations, or serving suggestions have not been
included in the calculations.

Recipes using raw or very lightly cooked eggs should be avoided by infants,
the elderly, pregnant women, convalescents, and anyone with a chronic
condition. Pregnant and breastfeeding women are advised to avoid eating
peanuts and peanut products. People with nut allergies should be aware
that some of the prepared ingredients used in the recipes in this book may
contain nuts. Always check the packaging before use.

CONTENTS

CHAPTER 4
SWEET PIES & PASTRIES 148

CHAPTER 5
BREAD & SAVORY 186

INTRODUCTION

Few types of cooking offer more rewards than home baking. Not only can you make irresistible sweet and savory treats for your family and friends, but the actual hands-on process of baking is immensely satisfying, and you may be surprised how much fun it can be. The basic skills are really easy to learn and you need very little in the way of special equipment to make some impressive cakes and other baked goods. All it needs is a little practice, and you'll get your baking confidence in no time!

While it's true that you can buy good-quality prepared cakes these days, the satisfaction of baking your own, knowing exactly what ingredients they contain, and even making them cheaper than you can buy them makes the effort all worthwhile. If you have children, baking is a great way to encourage them to start helping in the kitchen, and most children love to cook.

GETTING STARTED

Choosing bakeware

If you bake regularly, it helps to have a basic selection of cake pans.

- Baking/cookie sheets
- Deep round and square pans, 7–9 inches/18–23 cm
- 2–3 shallow, round layer cake pans, 7–8 inches/18–20
- Rectangular pan, about 8 x 12 inches/20 x 30 cm
- Springform round pan, 8–9 inches/20–23 cm
- Loaf pans, 8 x 4 x 2 inches/ 20 x 10 x 5 cm and 9 x 5 x 3 inches/23 x 13 x 8 cm
- 12-cup muffin pan
- Loose-bottom tart pan, 8–9 inches/20–23 cm

Fancy pans, such as ring pans, angel food cake pans, madeleine pans, or Bundt pans, can be added as required. Successful baking needs good-quality bakeware that will conduct the heat efficiently and evenly to cake batters and will last for years without rusting or warping. Stainless steel pans are long lasting and will not warp, while aluminum is cheaper but less durable. Nonstick pans can make for easy turning out, but they may not be as durable as uncoated pans. Flexible silicone bakeware is a good alternative to traditional metal pans, but can be expensive.

Why it's important to use the correct pan

If possible, always use the pan size stated in the recipe, because cooking times have been calculated for the stated pan, and if you change it to a different-size pan, the cake may cook unevenly and give a disappointing result.

What to do if you don't have the correct pan

If you don't have the right pan for the recipe, you don't necessarily have to rush out and buy a new one. Unless it's a particularly unusual shape, most cake pans can be changed for one of the same capacity without harm.

If the recipe uses a round pan but you prefer to use a square one, the square pan should be 1 inch/2.5 cm smaller than the round one. So if the recipe calls for a 9-inch/23-cm round pan, you can substitute an 8-inch/ 20-cm square one instead.

EQUIPMENT

OVEN

A reliable oven is essential to successful baking, and it's a good idea to check yours regularly with an oven thermometer to make sure it's accurate. Preheat the oven to the required temperature for 10–15 minutes before use, so that it has time to fully reach the correct temperature. Fan ovens cook more quickly than conventional ovens, so cooking times can be reduced by 5–10 minutes per hour, or the temperature may be reduced slightly.

Avoid the temptation to keep opening the oven door to check on your cake, particularly early in the cooking time, because a sudden rush of cold air may cause the cake to sink.

MEASURING CUPS

Metal and ceramic measuring cups are useful for measuring dry ingredients but less easy to use for liquids. Transparent glass or plastic cups are a good choice for measuring liquids, but make sure that they are heatproof. Choose ones with a good pouring lip and clear markings. Place the cup on a flat surface at eye level for accurate measuring of liquid ingredients.

Dry measuring cups are available in nested sets and usually include 2-cup, 1-cup, ½-cup, ⅓-cup, and ¼-cup sizes, and sometimes a ⅛-cup (2-tablespoon) size. Although butter and brown sugar should be packed tightly into a measuring cup, all other ingredients should be placed into a measuring cup loosely. Unless otherwise stated, the ingredients in the cups should be level—you can use the straight back edge of a knife or your fingers to level off the ingredients.

MEASURING SPOONS

It's important to use standard measuring spoons, measured level unless stated otherwise, because ordinary kitchen tablespoons and teaspoons can vary in size. In all the recipes in this book, a teaspoon is assumed to hold 5 ml and a tablespoon is assumed to hold 15 ml.

ELECTRIC MIXER/FOOD PROCESSOR

A handheld electric mixer with a powerful motor can be used for creaming, whisking, blending, and kneading. Tabletop mixers, with greater capacity and more power, are useful for all mixtures, particularly large quantities.

Food processors can cream, blend, or knead, as well as doing other cooking tasks. Again, choose one with a powerful motor for durability. Be careful when using a food processor or powerful electric mixer for making cakes because they mix the ingredients very quickly. It is important not to overbeat cake batters because this will make their texture too dense.

Food processors are unsuitable for mixing meringues because the enclosed bowl does not hold enough air to give them volume.

SPOONS

Wooden spoons are useful for creaming and mixing. Make sure you keep separate those used for cooking strongly flavored foods, such as onions, because wood can absorb flavors and may transfer them to more delicate mixtures.

Heat-resistant nylon spoons are durable and less prone to absorbing flavors. A large metal spoon is useful for folding in ingredients.

SPATULA

You'll find a flexible rubber or silicone spatula helpful for

light mixing and scraping out bowls cleanly. Some have a spoon-shaped blade, which helps when transferring cake batter from the bowl to the pan.

BOWLS

Different-size mixing bowls are essential, and a set of toughened glass bowls is a good basic start because they are durable, heatproof, and easy to clean. Melamine resin, plastic, and ceramic bowls often have pouring lips, and some have nonslip bottoms to grip the counter.

WIRE COOLING RACKS

A wire rack lets your cakes cool evenly and prevents condensation, which can cause soggy texture and poor keeping quality. They vary from a simple metal rectangle to expanding three-tier ones, which are useful for large batches of baking. Some have a nonstick coating for easier cleaning.

SIFTER/STRAINER

A good-quality rustproof metal sifter with a triggerlike handle or crank is useful for sifting together dry ingredients evenly. Or use a stainless steel or nylon strainer, which sometimes come in a set of three. Even nylon ones are hard wearing and will stand boiling water, but metal ones are the most durable and will last for years.

GRATERS

A hard-wearing stainless steel box grater or flat "Microplane" type grater with a firm grip handle is good for grating citrus rind, cheese, apple, chocolate, nutmeg, etc. You'll need a fine, medium, and coarse grater. Some also have a slicing option.

CITRUS SQUEEZER/ REAMER

A sturdy plastic, metal, toughened glass, or ceramic squeezer is used for extracting juice from citrus fruits. For smooth juice, you'll need one with a filter part to extract all the fibers from the juice. A wooden reamer squeezes out the juice by simply pushing into the halved fruit, but you may also get some seeds.

ROLLING PIN

For rolling pie and cookie doughs, a wooden rolling pin is a good tool and you can shape and cool tuiles on it, too. Marble, granite, or glass are more expensive but their cool smooth surface is good for rolling sticky mixtures.

PASTRY BRUSH

A pastry brush is the easiest way to grease cake pans evenly, and can also be used for applying glazes. They are available with natural bristles or more durable synthetic bristles.

COOKIE CUTTERS

A set of round cookie cutters, with either plain or fluted edges, is a good basic choice, preferably in metal. Later you can add fancy-shaped cutters. Make sure the cutting edge is sharp and the top edge is rolled to safeguard your fingers and keep the cutter rigid.

PASTRY BAG AND TIPS

For decorative piping of frostings or soft mixtures, you'll need pastry bags and tips. Strong nylon or fabric bags are washable and reusable, or you can buy strong disposable bags to save work. A small selection of stainless steel tips should include a plain writing, small and large star, and plain large vegetable tips.

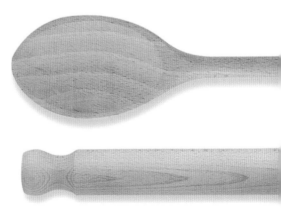

INGREDIENTS

FLOUR

Wheat flour is the most commonly used flour for baking. The amount of gluten (protein) in wheat flour varies between the different types:

All-purpose flour has the bran and wheat germ removed, and is then fortified with vitamins. Soft all-purpose flour is made from wheat with a low gluten content. It has a fine texture and is ideal for making cakes, pie dough, and cookies. White bread flour is milled from wheat with a high gluten content and is used for breads and most yeast cooking.

Self-rising flour is all-purpose white flour with baking powder added as a raising agent. To make self-rising flour add 2 teaspoons of baking powder to each scant 1⅝ cups all-purpose flour.

Whole wheat flour is flour that has been milled from the whole of the wheat grain. It is coarser and heavier than white flour. It is available as a strong (high-gluten) flour for bread making and a soft (lower-gluten) flour for cakes and pastry.

Other flours, such as brown flour, malted flour, corn flour, and buckwheat, rye, rice, and chestnut flours, are also sometimes used to a limited extent in baking, each having its own unique characteristic or flavor.

SUGARS

Most sugar is produced from one of two sources: sugar cane or sugar beet. There are a number of different types of sugar, each with its own particular qualities. Unrefined sugars are made from sugar cane and have a higher mineral, vitamin, and trace element content than refined sugars.

Granulated sugar can be used to achieve a crunchy texture in some cookies and in cakes prepared by the rubbing-in method.

Superfine sugar has a finer crystal and dissolves more readily. It is the type of sugar most frequently used in baking. It is also known as caster sugar because it is suitable for placing in a caster—a container with a perforated top, similar to a flour sifter. Because it dissolves readily, it is perfect for making meringues. It can be substituted for granulated sugar cup for cup.

granulated sugar, superfine, and **confectioners' sugar** are unrefined forms of the refined sugars.

Molasses sugar is a dark, fine-grained unrefined sugar from Mauritius that is used for rich fruit cakes. This unique sugar contains the highest amount of natural molasses of any sugar, resulting in an extra rich flavor and moistness. Molasses syrup is the dark-colored syrup that is left over after sugar has been refined. It is very concentrated, so only a small amount is required. Store molasses in tightly sealed containers at room temperature or in the refrigerator.

Raw brown sugar is a large, coarse-grained brown sugar that can be made from either refined or unrefined sugar. As well as being used in baking, it is sometimes sprinkled over the tops of pies, crumbles, and cakes for its crunchy texture.

Light and **dark brown sugars** are usually refined white sugar that has been tossed in molasses or syrup. The darker the sugar, the stronger the molasses flavor.

Confectioners' sugar has a fine, powdery grain and dissolves almost instantly. It is used in some cookies and pastry, and for making frostings and fillings.

FATS

Butter produces the best flavor. Unsalted butter is generally considered best for baking. If you do use salted butter, you will not need to add any extra salt to the recipe (except for bread making). Use butter straight from the refrigerator for pastry making and at room temperature for cake making.

Margarine is preferred over butter by some people for baking. Block margarine is generally the best to use, but soft margarine is needed when making cakes by the all-in-one method.

Low-fat spreads are not suitable for baking, because they contain a high proportion of water.

Suet is used for making suet crust pastry and can be made from either shredded beef fat or solidified vegetable oils.

Shortening and white vegetable fat have a bland flavor, but give a light, short texture to pastry and cookies, so are sometimes used. They are usually combined with butter for flavor.

EGGS

The size of eggs used in baking is important. Store eggs in the refrigerator away from strong-smelling foods. Remove from the refrigerator to return to room temperature before using if possible, because cold eggs do not combine as well with other ingredients or trap as much air.

RAISING AGENTS

Baking powder is a mixture of cream of tartar and baking soda. When mixed with moisture, it releases carbon dioxide, a harmless gas that expands during baking to make the food rise.

Baking soda produces carbon dioxide when mixed with an acid, such as lemon juice or buttermilk. It should always be mixed with other dry ingredients before the liquid is added.

Yeast is a single-cell organism that converts the natural sugars in flour to produce carbon dioxide. Yeast needs warmth, moisture, and food (sugars) to work. It is available in both dried and fresh forms for baking.

GREASING & LINING TINS

For many simple sponge cakes, you just need to give the bottom and sides of the tin a quick brush of oil or melted butter and insert a piece of nonstick parchment paper in the bottom. Richer or low-fat batters usually need a thoroughly greased and lined tin to prevent sticking.

Lining a round tin

1. Grease the tin. Cut a strip of parchment paper about 1 inch/2.5 cm longer than the circumference and about 1 inch/2.5 cm deeper than the tin.
2. Fold up one long edge about ½ inch/1 cm, then unfold, leaving a crease.
3. Use scissors to snip cuts along the folded edge of the paper so that it can be eased into the tin to fit around the curve at the bottom.
4. Place the tin on a sheet of parchment paper and draw around it with a pencil to mark the size. Cut with scissors just inside the line, making a round to fit inside the bottom, covering the snipped edges of the side lining paper. Grease the paper.

Lining a square tin

1. Grease the tin. Cut a strip of parchment paper about 1 inch/2.5 cm longer than the circumference of the tin and 1 inch/2.5 cm deeper.
2. Fold up one long edge about ½ inch/1 cm, then unfold, leaving a crease. Fit the paper into the sides of the tin, cutting a diagonal slit into the folded edge to fit each corner.
3. Place the tin on a sheet of parchment paper, draw around it to mark the size, then cut just inside the line to make a square. Lay the square inside the tin, covering the folded edges. Grease the paper.

Lining a jelly roll tin and sheet tin

1. Grease the bottom and sides of the tin. Cut a piece of parchment paper 2¾ inches/7 cm larger than the tin.
2. Place the tin on the paper, then make a cut from each corner of the paper in toward the tin corner.
3. Place the paper inside the tin so that the diagonally cut corners overlap and fit neatly. Grease the paper.

Lining a loaf tin

1. Grease the tin. Cut a strip of parchment paper the length of the tin bottom and wide enough to cover the bottom and long sides. Place the paper in the tin.
2. Cut a second piece of parchment paper the width of the tin bottom and long enough to cover the bottom and ends of the tin. Slot this in over the first piece to line the tin, then grease the paper.

Flouring tins

1. Grease the bottom and sides of the tin, then slip a piece of parchment paper in the bottom. Grease the paper.
2. Sprinkle a little flour into the tin. Tilt the tin, tapping lightly so the flour coats the bottom and sides evenly. Tip out any excess.

ESSENTIAL RECIPES: **CAKES**

The main ingredients for making cakes are flour, fat, sugar, and eggs. The proportion of fat to flour will influence the method by which the cake is made. With half or less fat to flour, the rubbing-in method is used, while with half or more fat to flour, the creaming method is used. If little or no fat is used, then whisking is the appropriate method.

CREAMED CAKES

The most well-known of cakes made by this method is the Sponge Cake, which uses butter, sugar, eggs, and flour in equal quantities to make a light and airy cake. It makes a good base for many variations. Cakes made by this method should have a light, even texture. The higher the proportion of fat, sugar, and eggs to flour, the richer the cake will be.

Sponge Cake

- ¾ CUP UNSALTED BUTTER, SOFTENED
- SCANT 1 CUP SUPERFINE SUGAR
- 3 EGGS, BEATEN
- SCANT 1¼ CUPS SELF-RISING FLOUR

BASIC METHOD

1 Cream (beat) the fat and sugar together in a bowl until pale and fluffy. A wooden spoon or a handheld electric mixer is ideal for this task. The more thoroughly the fat and sugar are creamed together, the lighter the texture of the cake will be. Creaming also breaks down the sugar crystals, giving a finer texture. Use sugar with small crystals, such as superfine or light brown sugar, rather than the coarser

granulated or raw brown sugar, because these will blend with the fat more easily.

2 Gradually add the eggs, beating well after each addition. Eggs are best used at room temperature. Add any flavoring extracts at this stage.

3 Sift the flour and any other fine dry ingredients. Carefully fold into the cake batter. Use a large metal spoon or a spatula to do this and be careful to incorporate the flour gently without knocking out the air you have beaten into the batter. Use a cutting and folding-over movement.

Storage Cakes made by the creaming method keep well in an airtight container. Undecorated cakes freeze well.

ALL-IN-ONE CAKES
This is a simplified variation of the creaming method. All the ingredients are beaten together at once until smooth. Extra baking powder helps to make the cake rise and soft margarine or butter is essential for it to mix fully. This gives a close-textured cake and is an ideal method when time is of the essence.

WHISKED SPONGE CAKES
Whisked sponges depend on the amount of air trapped into the eggs and sugar during the whisking of the eggs. The bowl should be warmed and the eggs at room temperature. The best results are achieved by using an electric mixer. Care then has to be taken not to knock the air out when folding in the flour, which must be done with a lightness of hand.

CURDLING IN CAKE BATTER
Curdling is the term used when the water from the eggs separates out from the fat globules in the cake batter, and is usually caused by the eggs being too cold. A curdled cake batter will hold less air and will produce a cake with a dense texture. To help prevent curdling, use eggs at room temperature. If your batter does begin to curdle, beat in a tablespoon of the flour to help bind the mixture back together. This is not a true curdling, which is the process of separating the curds from the whey in milk.

Jelly Roll Cake

- 3 LARGE EGGS
- SCANT ⅔ CUP SUPERFINE SUGAR
- SCANT 1 CUP ALL-PURPOSE FLOUR
- 1 TBSP HOT WATER

BASIC METHOD

1 Put the eggs and sugar in a warmed bowl and whisk together until very pale and thick. Air will become entangled with the albumen in the egg white and the mixture will increase considerably in volume. A good test to see if you have whisked in enough air is to try to write your initials with the mixture dropping from the whisk. If the mixture holds its shape long enough for you to write two initials before they disappear, the mixture is thick enough. Setting the bowl over a pan of hot water can help speed up the process.

2 If the mixture has been whisked over hot water, remove from the heat and continue whisking until it is cool.

3 Carefully fold in the sifted flour with a large metal spoon or spatula using a cutting and folding-over movement, blending with a little water.

4 Drizzle over any melted butter or oil specified in the recipe and carefully fold in.

Storage Fat-free sponges are best eaten on the day they are made. Those with some fat will keep a little longer if stored in an airtight container.

3 Stir in the sugar and any other dry ingredients used to flavor the scone, such as coconut or fruit.

4 Stir in the egg and milk.

Storage Rubbed-in cakes, such as scones should be kept for no more than three days, because they tend to become dry over time.

RUBBED-IN CAKES

This method of cake mixing produces a plain, coarse texture and is often used for breads and biscuits. The proportion of fat to flour varies from 25 percent to around 66 percent. Rubbing in the fat with the fingertips held high over the bowl incorporates air. Liquid is added and the mixture is then gently brought together. Be careful not to overwork the batter or the results will be tough.

Scone Mixture

- SCANT 1⅝ CUPS SELF-RISING FLOUR
- 6 TBSP UNSALTED BUTTER, CUT INTO SMALL PIECES
- 1 TBSP SUPERFINE SUGAR
- PINCH OF SALT
- 1 EGG, BEATEN
- ¼ CUP MILK

BASIC METHOD

1 Sift the flour into a bowl.

2 Rub in the fat with your fingertips, lifting your hands high to help to incorporate air into the mixture. The mixture should resemble fine breadcrumbs.

MELTED CAKES

A few dense, moist cakes, such as gingerbread, employ this method. The fat and sugar are melted together before the dry ingredients are stirred in.

Gingerbread

- 3¼ CUPS ALL-PURPOSE FLOUR
- 1–2 TSP BAKING SODA
- 2–4 TSP GROUND GINGER
- 1 CUP UNSALTED BUTTER
- SCANT 1 CUP SUGAR (MOLASSES OR SYRUP)

BASIC METHOD

1 Sift the flour, raising agent, and ginger into a bowl.

2 Melt the fat, sugar, and/or syrup in a pan over low heat until the mixture combines. Be careful not to overheat.

3 Pour into the dry ingredients along with any other liquids that are used.

4 Beat to form a smooth batter consistency.

Storage These cakes are best if left for one day before eating to become moist. They keep well in an airtight container.

SMALL CAKES

The same basic principles and techniques for making large cakes also apply to small cakes. However, the oven temperature is usually higher and the baking time much shorter. Small cakes, each not much more than a couple of bites in size, can be cooked in a 12-hole mini muffin pan. For more substantial individual cakes, a muffin pan can be used. Lining the pans with paper cake liners will ensure that they turn out easily. Some small cakes are made as one large cake and then cut into appropriately sized bars or squares. This is a quick way of producing individual cakes. Small cakes should be simply decorated or left plain.

IS IT COOKED?

Follow the timings in the recipe as a guideline, but also rely on your own judgment, because ovens vary in temperature. Small cakes should be well risen, firm, and springy to the touch, and sponge cakes should also be springy to the touch.

Test by gently pressing the cake with a finger. Once you have removed your finger, the cake should spring back, but if you can still see the fingerprint, return the cake to the oven for a few minutes longer. Fruit cake and deep sponge cakes are best tested with a skewer inserted into the center. The skewer will come out clean when the cake is cooked.

For most cakes, let cool for a few minutes in the pan before turning out and transferring to a cooling rack to cool completely. Some cakes, such as rich fruit cakes, benefit from being left to cool completely in the pan—the recipe will specify this where necessary.

ESSENTIAL RECIPES: PASTRY

Basic pie dough is not as difficult to make as is sometimes perceived, and although preparing other, more special pastries is an area of baking that does require a certain amount of skill, by following the recipes closely, that skill can be acquired and professional results achieved with a little practice.

It is important to follow a few basic rules when making pie dough. Always measure the ingredients accurately and keep everything cool. Always use a light touch and handle the dough with care. Knead the dough just sufficiently to bind it together—over-kneading will start to develop the gluten in the flour and result in a tough, greasy pastry. Roll out pie dough lightly, being careful not to stretch it unduly. Use only a small amount of flour when rolling out to avoid upsetting the careful balance of ingredients. Let the dough rest wrapped in the refrigerator before rolling. A little salt may be added to bring out the flavor of pastry, but if salted butter or margarine is used, this is usually sufficient.

COOKING PIE DOUGH

The oven must be hot when the pie dough is first put in so that it will rise when the air that it contains is heated. The gluten in the flour absorbs the water and stretches and entangles the air in the dough as the air expands. The heat of the oven then sets the pastry in its risen shape. As it cooks, the starch grains in the flour will also burst and absorb the fat. If the oven is too cool, the fat will melt and run

out while the flour remains uncooked, resulting in a heavy, soggy, and greasy pastry. After the pastry is set, the temperature can be reduced to cook the filling, if required.

TYPES OF PASTRY

All kinds of pastry, except suet crust, use all-purpose flour. Whole wheat flour can be used instead of white, but it produces heavier results and requires extra liquid to bring it together.

Flaky Pastry

Perhaps the most common home-baked pastry, this is also one of the easiest to master as long as the basic rules of pastry making are followed. A proportion of half fat to flour is used.

- 8 TBSP UNSALTED BUTTER
- SCANT 1⅝ CUPS ALL-PURPOSE FLOUR
- 2–3 TBSP COLD WATER

BASIC METHOD

1 Sift the flour into a bowl.

2 Cut the fat into small cubes and add to the flour. Rub in using your fingertips, lifting your hand high above the bowl to incorporate more air. The mixture will resemble fine breadcrumbs when the fat has been fully rubbed in.

3 Stir in any additional flavorings, if using, such as ground nuts, cheese, or sugar, for sweet pastry.

4 Add the liquid all at once and use your fingers to bring the dough together. Turn the dough out onto a lightly floured counter and knead very lightly. Ideally, the dough should be wrapped in foil or plastic wrap and chilled in the refrigerator for 30 minutes to let the dough "relax," which helps to prevent it from

shrinking when it is baked.

5 Roll out the dough on a lightly floured counter. Rolling should be carried out in short, sharp strokes, with a light, even pressure in a forward movement only. Turn the dough as you roll.

6 Use as required, then let the dough relax again in a cool place for 15–30 minutes before baking. This is especially important if you have not previously relaxed the dough.

7 Bake in a hot oven for 15–20 minutes, until set. The temperature may then be reduced.

Short-crust pastry can be made in a food processor, which helps keep it cooler than warm hands. Put the flour and fat in the processor and

process until the mixture resembles fine breadcrumbs. The liquid can then be added to the machine, processing until the dough comes together. Alternatively, for greater control, tip the flour and fat mixture into a bowl and add the liquid by hand. The proportion of fat to flour can be increased, or eggs added to produce richer pastries, such as pâté sucrée. Because of the increased fat content, these pastries can be more difficult to handle. In some cases, the fat content is so high that additional liquid is not needed to bring the dough together. Rolling out these extra-rich pastries can be made easier by rolling the dough between two sheets of plastic wrap. Additional ingredients, such as ground nuts, lemon rind, sugar, or spices, can be added for flavor.

BAKING BLIND

When used to line a pan, flaky pastry is often precooked to set the dough before the filling is added. The term used to describe this is "baking blind."

1 Line the pan with the rolled-out dough and prick the bottom with a fork.

2 Chill for about 30 minutes in the refrigerator or 10 minutes in the freezer (you can also bake pastry shells blind from frozen).

3 Line the pastry shell with a sheet of nonstick parchment paper, wax paper, or foil and fill with purpose-made ceramic or metal pie weights or use dried beans or rice. These baking beans help to conduct heat and cook the dough, as well as preventing the dough from puffing up in the center.

4 Bake for 10 minutes, then remove the paper and weights and bake for an additional 10 minutes, until the pastry is just golden.

5 Remove from the oven and brush a little beaten egg or egg white over the bottom to seal (the heat of the pastry will cook the egg).

Puff Pastry

Both flaky and puff pastry are more difficult to make and very time consuming, but their richness, especially in the case of puff pastry, gives them a superior flavor. More experienced bakers will enjoy the challenge of making these pastries as well as the end results. Puff pastry has the highest proportion of fat to flour and is therefore the most difficult to handle. The principle behind the pastry is to create many layers of dough and butter by folding and turning the two together. For an evenly layered pastry, it is important that you always roll it to the same thickness and that the edges are very straight and even.

- SCANT 2½ CUPS ALL-PURPOSE FLOUR
- ¾ CUP UNSALTED BUTTER
- 8 TBSP COLD WATER

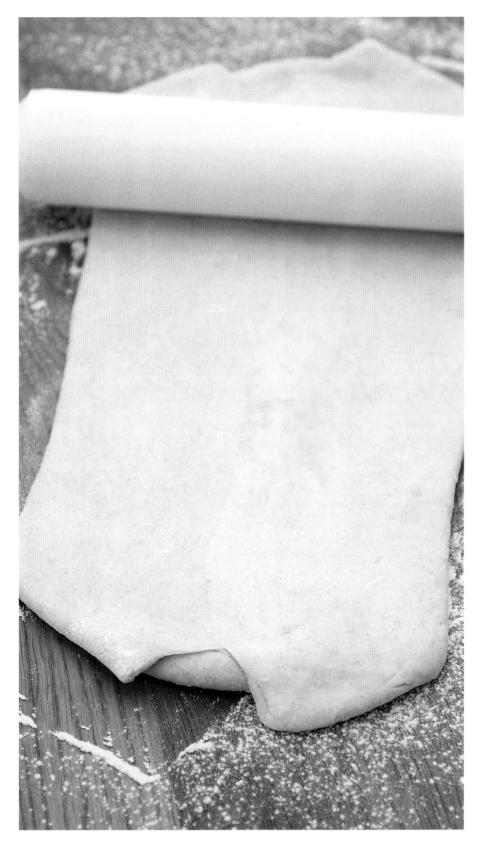

BASIC METHOD

1 Sift the flour into a bowl and rub in one quarter of the butter.

2 Add the water and use your fingers to bring the dough together. Knead briefly to form a smooth dough. Put in a plastic bag and chill in the refrigerator for 30 minutes.

3 Roll out the remaining butter between 2 sheets of plastic wrap to form a block about ½ inch/ 1 cm thick.

4 Roll out the dough to a square about 4 times the size of the block of butter.

5 Put the block of butter in the center of the dough and fold over the corners of the dough to completely enclose the butter.

6 Roll out the dough into a rectangle 3 times as long as it is wide.

7 Fold one third of the dough over to cover the middle third, then fold the remainder over the top.

8 Give the dough a half turn, roll out to form another rectangle, and fold again as before. Repeat the initial rolling and folding 6 times in total, chilling the dough frequently between rolling.

9 Let relax for a final 30 minutes, then use as required. Trim the folded edges of the dough before using to assist the rising. Bake in a hot oven. The pastry should rise 6–8 times its original height.

3 Roll out the dough into a rectangle 3 times as long as it is wide.

4 Dot one-third of the remaining fat over two-thirds of the dough in rough lumps. Fold the uncovered dough over to cover half the fatted dough, then fold the remaining third over the top.

5 Seal the edges of the dough by pressing down with a rolling pin.

6 Give the dough a half turn, roll out to form another rectangle, and repeat steps 4 and 5 twice more until all the fat has been used. Put the dough in a plastic bag and chill in the refrigerator for 30 minutes.

7 Roll and fold the dough 3 more times as before, but without the addition of fat. Let relax for a final 30 minutes, then use as required. Trim the folded edges of the dough before using to assist the rising. Bake in a hot oven.

Flaky (filo) Pastry

This uses a slightly lower proportion of fat to flour—two thirds to three quarters fat to flour—and the fat is added in stages. It is advisable to use a white bread flour for flaky pastry. After the initial fat has been added, the dough is kneaded to develop the elasticity of the gluten, resulting in an elastic dough that will rise easily. A little lemon juice is added to help develop the gluten and counteract the richness of the pastry. The dough must be left to relax before being baked. Once cooked, the pastry does not keep long unless frozen, although the uncooked dough can be stored in the refrigerator for up to 48 hours. Uncooked dough can also be sealed and frozen for up to four months.

- SCANT 1⅝ CUPS ALL-PURPOSE FLOUR
- ¾ CUP UNSALTED BUTTER
- 6–7 TBSP COLD MILK OR WATER

BASIC METHOD

1 Sift the flour into a bowl and rub in one quarter of the fat.

2 Add the water and use your fingers to bring the mixture together. Knead briefly to form a smooth dough.

Rough Puff

This pastry is relatively easy to make and produces a fabulous light, flaky pastry. It can be a little sticky to handle to begin with. It has a similar fat content to flaky pastry.

- SCANT 1⅝ CUPS ALL-PURPOSE FLOUR
- ¾ CUP UNSALTED BUTTER
- 6–7 TBSP COLD MILK OR WATER

BASIC METHOD

1 Sift the four into a bowl and add the fat cut into small squares or lumps.

2 Add the water and use your fingers to bring the dough together. Knead very lightly.

3 Roll and fold the dough as for puff pastry.

Suet Crust Pastry

Suet crust pastry is a filling, homely kind of pastry. Self-rising flour or all-purpose flour and baking powder is used to make this.

- SCANT 1⅝ CUPS ALL-PURPOSE FLOUR
- 5 OZ/150 G SUET (BEFORE SHREDDING)
- 2 TSP BAKING POWDER
- ⅔ CUP COLD WATER

BASIC METHOD

1 Sift the flour into a bowl.

2 Shred the suet, then stir it and the baking powder into the flour.

3 Add enough water to form an elastic dough.

4 Only roll out the dough once to avoid producing a hard pastry.

COVERING A PIE

This is the basic method for making a single crust to cover a savory or sweet pie filling. You can then add decorative details and a glaze to enhance the appearance of the pie.

1 Roll out the pie dough to about 2 inches/5 cm larger all around the top of the dish.

2 Cut a strip about 1 inch/ 2.5 cm wide from the edge of the dough.

3 Moisten the edge of the dish and stick the dough strip to the dish.

4 Fill the pie and dampen the dough strip with a little water.

5 Using a rolling pin, carefully lift the dough over the pie. Press the edge down to seal.

6 Using a sharp knife, trim the edge and make a small hole in the center of the pie to let the steam escape.

Hot Watercrust Pastry

This traditional type of pastry is used for raised pies, such as pork or game pies. It is the exception to one of the basic rules of pastry making in that its success depends on the warmth of the utensils and flour throughout the making and shaping. If it becomes too cold, it will be difficult to handle.

- SCANT 1 CUP ALL-PURPOSE FLOUR
- 3 OZ/85 G SHORTENING
- 5 TBSP WATER

Choux Pastry

This is a rich, soft pastry that relies predominately on its high water content, which becomes very hot during cooking to form a hollow pastry shell.

- SCANT ⅝ CUP WHITE BREAD FLOUR
- 4 TBSP UNSALTED BUTTER
- ⅔ CUP WATER
- 2 EGGS

BASIC METHOD

1 Sift the flour into a bowl and make a well in the center.

2 Put the shortening and water in a pan and heat until the fat melts, then bring to a boil. Immediately add to the well in the flour and mix with a spoon to form a dough, then knead the dough.

3 The dough should be shaped while still warm and cooked in a hot oven.

BASIC METHOD

1 Sift the flour.

2 Put the butter and water in a pan and heat until the fat melts.

3 Add the flour to the pan all at once and beat with a wooden spoon until the mixture forms a ball around the spoon. Let cool slightly.

4 Gradually beat in the eggs until the dough is smooth and glossy. The more the mixture is beaten, the better the results, because more air is incorporated.

5 Shape by piping or spoon, as required. Bake in a hot oven.

PASTRY FINISHES

- Use a blunt knife to tap the edge of the pie and raise it. This also helps to seal the pie fully.
- Press the edge with a floured fork.
- Press one thumb around the edge while you pinch the outside edge between your other thumb and index finger.
- Press a thumb around the edge and draw a knife in a short distance from the edge toward the center of the pie between each thumbprint to create a scalloped edge.
- Decorate the pie by using the pastry trimmings. Cut them into leaves or other shapes, as desired, and stick to the pie crust by moistening slightly.

GLAZES

Glazing the dough will produce a shiny golden surface once baked. You can use milk, beaten egg mixed with a little water, or lightly beaten egg white for glazing. Brush a thin layer over the dough with a pastry brush, but avoid making the dough too wet. For sweet pies, a little superfine sugar can also be sprinkled on top.

ESSENTIAL RECIPES: COOKIES

From the flat, thin wafer to the traditionally chunky chocolate chip cookie, you can find a cookie that is perfect for just about any occasion, be it a decadent coffee morning, hearty afternoon tea, an elegant dinner or a packed lunch on the run. As might be guessed from the numerous styles of cookies, there are several methods for preparing them.

Because cookies cook quickly, you will need to keep a close eye on the baking until you become more experienced in gauging the exact cooking time easily. For most cookies, let cool on the cookie sheet for a few minutes before transferring to a cooling rack to cool completely. Many cookies are very soft when they come out of the oven but become crisp on cooling, so remember to remove them from the pan before they become completely cold or they may stick. Store in an airtight container to retain freshness and crispness. Most cookies also freeze well—simply thaw at room temperature.

Rolled and Molded Cookies

Here the cookie dough is rolled out and cut out or shaped into logs, balls, or crescents. Be careful not to add too much extra flour when rolling and shaping, because this will alter the careful balance of the ingredients. If a dough is very soft, you may find it easier to roll out between two sheets of plastic wrap. Try to avoid rerolling too many times, or the cookies may become tough.

Drop Cookies

These are the quickest and easiest to make. They are often made by the creaming method, where the fat and sugar are beaten together, then the flour and any additional flavorings, such as nuts or chocolate chips, are added. The mixture is then beaten just enough to bring all the ingredients together in a soft dough, which can then be dropped onto the cookie sheet from spoons. Always place well spaced apart on the cookie sheet, because the cookies will spread during baking.

Piped cookies

Some cookies are piped from a plain or fluted pastry tip to produce a decorative effect. The consistency of the cookie dough needs to be just right—too stiff and the dough will be hard to pipe; too soft and the cookies will lose their shape when baked.

Wafers

Some classic cookies are very thin and crisp. The mixture is very soft (that of a batter) and is spooned onto a cookie sheet and spread out to form a circle. These are probably the hardest cookies to bake, because they bake very rapidly. They are sometimes shaped into rolls or curled. In this case, you need to work fast, only baking a couple at a time, because they need to be shaped while still warm.

Sliced cookies

The dough in this instance is firm and can be shaped into a log. The individual cookies are then sliced at the desired thickness. The uncooked cookie dough can be stored in the refrigerator for several days and a few cookies cut and baked from the log as desired. This is an ideal way of making freshly baked cookies every day.

ESSENTIAL RECIPES: BREADS & YEAST

There are so many different kinds of homemade bread that they can easily fill a book in themselves. Many, like soda bread, plain white bread, malt bread, and rolls are great basics, but once mastered, the temptation to move on to making delicious flavored breads is hard to resist. Not all breads rely on yeast as a raising agent and you will find a selection of breads made without yeast in this book.

Yeast cooking is not particularly difficult and the results are most rewarding. In contrast to working with pie dough, a warm kitchen will help you on the way. Also, there is no need for the caution in handling that pie dough requires—a firm hand is perfect for kneading the dough to develop the gluten content of the bread, which gives it its unique texture. Of course, you do need to leave more time to produce yeasted products, but for the most part they can be left alone to rise while you are free to do other things.

Most yeasted breads and bakes freeze well, so when time is plentiful, they are ideal for batch baking. The frozen bakes can be thawed at room temperature and refreshed in a hot oven for 5 minutes to warm through before serving.

TYPES OF YEAST

Yeast is the raising agent most frequently used for breads. It is a living organism that, when active, creates carbon dioxide. Small bubbles of carbon dioxide then become trapped within the structure of the dough, giving bread its characteristic structure. There are two main types of bread yeasts available: fresh and dried.

Fresh Yeast

This can be purchased from health food stores and some bakeries. It has a creamy color and is moist and firm. Fresh yeast is usually dissolved in the liquid and left for a preliminary fermentation before being added to the remaining ingredients. It will only keep for a few days in the refrigerator, but can be frozen for up to three months.

Dried Yeast

This is available in two forms. Regular dried yeast requires a preliminary

GLUTEN

Gluten is formed by a combination of two proteins, gliadin and glutenin, which are found in wheat flour. Bread flours have a higher proportion of these proteins than normal flour. When these proteins are hydrated, they bond with each other, creating a large protein called gluten that gives the bread its structure. The longer the dough is kneaded, the stronger the gluten becomes and the better texture the bread has. It is possible to knead the dough so much that it becomes too warm and the gluten begins to break down, but this is very unlikely to happen if kneading by hand. If you choose to knead in a mixer, knead for short bursts, resting it a few seconds each time for the dough to cool slightly.

fermentation and is activated by mixing with a little liquid and sugar or flour.

Active dry yeast, fast-action dried yeast, and instant dried yeast are just different names for yeast that does not require this preliminary fermentation and is simply stirred into the flour before the liquid is added. The first rising and punching down can also be eliminated if time is short. Dried yeast has a longer shelf life than fresh yeast and does not need to be refrigerated.

EFFECTS OF TEMPERATURE ON YEAST

Yeast works quickest in warm temperatures, so it is generally recommended that the dough is left in a warm place to rise. However, yeast does not stop working at lower temperatures—it simply slows down. Therefore, dough can be made, shaped, and then left to rise overnight in a refrigerator. Let the dough return to room temperature before baking. Yeast that is left to work in slower conditions produces a loaf that many people regard as having more flavor and character.

EFFECTS OF OTHER INGREDIENTS ON YEAST ACTION

A basic loaf consists of just flour, yeast, salt, and water, but some breads as well as cakes and even pastries are made with yeast doughs that have been enriched with other ingredients such as butter, sugar, and eggs. Additional ingredients may contribute to the rising, give added color to the crumb and crust, and may also improve the keeping qualities. However, all these additional ingredients will have an effect on the action of yeast.

Sugar in small amounts speeds up the action of yeast, but in larger quantities—above 2 oz/55 g per 1 lb/450 g—it will retard the action of yeast.

Fat in proportions above 1 oz/25 g per 1 lb/450 g will retard the action of yeast.

Eggs, because of their fat content, may slow the action of yeast, but they also have the ability to retain air in the mixture, so often help to produce a lighter texture.

To overcome any adverse effects of these added ingredients:
- Leave additional time for the rising—2 hours or more is not unusual.
- Make the dough in two parts, with the additional ingredients added after an initial rising.
- Extra yeast may be added.

A NOTE ABOUT SALT

Salt is an essential ingredient in bread making, because it not only adds flavor but also strengthens the gluten structure, and helps control the growth of yeast. Too little and the result will be a poor gluten structure; too much and the salt will inhibit the action of the yeast. Both will result in a loaf of poor volume and flavor. For this reason, it is important not to vary the amount of salt in a recipe, even if you are trying to reduce your salt intake, because this will adversely affect the finished product.

MAKING YEAST BREADS
BASIC METHOD

The method used is basically the same for all yeast breads, although individual steps may vary according to the recipe.

- 4¾ CUPS WHITE BREAD FLOUR
- 2 TSP SALT
- 2 TSP ACTIVE DRY YEAST
- 2 TBSP OLIVE OIL OR BUTTER
- ABOUT 2 CUPS LUKEWARM WATER

1 Sift the flour and salt into a large bowl. Stir in the active dry yeast, and make a well in the center. Pour in the liquid and mix to a soft, slightly sticky dough.

2 Turn out the dough onto a lightly floured counter and begin kneading by folding the dough over on top of itself and pushing away with the heal of your hand—do not be afraid to be forceful. Keep kneading, giving the dough a quarter turn as you do so, for 10 minutes, or until the dough is very smooth and elastic and no longer sticky. Alternatively, knead the dough in an electric mixer fitted with a dough hook for 6–8 minutes.

3 Form the dough into a ball and put in a lightly oiled bowl. Rub a little oil over the surface of the dough to prevent it from drying out, and cover loosely with plastic wrap or slide the bowl inside a clean plastic carrier bag. Let rise in a warm place for 1 hour, or until doubled in size.

4 When the dough has increased to double its original size, turn out onto a lightly floured work counter and lightly knead again for a few minutes. This is called "punching down," because some of the air that has been incorporated into the dough is punched out and the dough shrinks in size. This ensures that the bread has a more even texture, because any large air pockets are removed at this stage.

5 Shape the dough as required and place in a lightly greased loaf pan. The dough should fill the pan halfway.

6 Cover loosely again and let rise for a second time until doubled in size.

7 Bake in a hot oven. To test if the bread is cooked, turn out of the pan and tap the bottom. The loaf should sound hollow. Let cool on a cooling rack.

YEAST-FREE BREADS

Some breads do not contain yeast. These breads use another method to leaven the bread (make the bread rise) or are unleavened. Sometimes called quick breads, soda bread and cornbread fall into the former category. Baking soda or baking powder is added to the dough. These produce carbon dioxide, a process that begins as soon as the dough is mixed, so the bread must be baked immediately. The dough should be soft and sticky, and in some cases is more like a thick batter. Quick breads have a soft, crumbly texture and some are best served warm. Most are best eaten the day they are made.

Unleavened breads are sometimes called flat breads. Some flat breads, such as naan and pita bread are in fact leavened with yeast but unleavened dough can also be used. Flat breads are among the oldest breads. Evidence has been found that they were cooked on stones in Neolithic times. Paratha, tortillas, and chapatis are all examples of yeast-free flat breads. In the modern home, they can be cooked on a griddle or in a heavy-bottom skillet. Flat breads can be topped like pizza and focaccia, stuffed like pita bread, filled with beans and rice and rolled like chapatis or tortillas, or used for dipping like poppadums from India.

BREAD MACHINES

You can make bread with the minimum of fuss and effort by using a bread machine. Once all the ingredients have been weighed and added to the pan, the machine can be left to do the hard work and a few hours later you have a freshly baked loaf. Although some of the fun of making bread is removed, it is nevertheless a very convenient way of producing freshly baked, warm bread, and because most machines have a timer, you can set it so that you can enjoy it when you wake up in the morning. Always follow the manufacturer's instructions, because quantities of ingredients and methods may vary.

TOP TIPS FOR
SUCCESSFUL BAKING

Before you start

- Always preheat the oven to the correct temperature so it's ready to use when your cake is mixed. Leave at least 10 minutes for preheating.
- Grease pans lightly with a mild-flavored oil, such as sunflower oil, or melted butter. Use a pastry bush to cover the pan quickly and evenly.
- For creamed mixtures, such as layer cakes, line the bottom of the pan with nonstick parchment paper; for rich mixtures and fruit cakes, line the bottom and sides of the pan. For very rich fruit cakes, wrap a double thickness of brown paper around the outside of the pan for extra protection and tie with string to secure.
- If you don't have the correct-size pan for the recipe, or prefer to use an unusual shaped pan such as a heart-shaped pan, just match the capacity—for example, an 8-inch/20-cm round pan holds the same volume of liquid as a 7-inch/18-cm square pan.
- Assemble all your ingredients and measure everything before you start to mix.

The perfect mix

- Always sift the flour with raising agents or spices before adding to a mixture so that they are evenly distributed throughout the mix.
- If you run out of self-rising flour, add 2½ tsp baking powder to every 2 cups all-purpose flour and sift together thoroughly before use.
- Most cake recipes use either butter or hard (block) margarine, which are interchangeable although butter has a much better flavor. Soft (tub) margarines and oil are good for all-in-one recipes, but less successful for creamed methods. Low-fat spreads have a high water content and give poor results in conventional recipes.
- For most recipes, fats should be used at room temperature for ease of mixing. Hard butter or block margarine can be softened for a few seconds in the microwave to make mixing easier.
- It's best to use eggs at room temperature for baking because they give a better volume and hold more air when whisked. If you usually store your eggs in the refrigerator, remove them about 30 minutes before you start to mix.
- To separate eggs, tap the shell against the side of a mixing bowl to crack, then break open, letting the white run out into the bowl and holding the yolk in one half of the shell. Tip the yolk backward and forward from shell to shell to let all the white run into the bowl.
- When folding in flour, use a metal spoon, cutting through the mixture with a light, quick action to keep as much air in it as possible. Over-mixing can result in a heavy, close-textured cake.

Baked to perfection

- Unless otherwise stated, place your cake on the center shelf of the oven to bake. If your oven tends to cook more quickly at the back or sides, carefully turn the cake pan or cookie sheet around toward the end of the cooking time.
- Resist the temptation to open the oven door too often during cooking, and close it gently rather than banging it shut. It's best to try to wait until at least halfway through the cooking time before sneaking a look. A quick peep won't harm the cake, but if you open the door too often, the temperature will drop and this may prevent the cake from rising properly.
- To test light sponge cakes for doneness, press the top lightly with a fingertip—the cake should feel spongy to the touch and spring back when released. To check rich fruit cakes for doneness, listen closely—if the cake is still sizzling inside, it is not yet thoroughly cooked. Most large cakes will shrink slightly from the sides of the pan when they are cooked. As a final test, insert a toothpick or thin knife into the center of the cake, then lift it out. If the cake is cooked, it should come out clean; if it's sticky, the mixture needs more cooking.
- Most cakes should be cooled slightly in the pan before turning out, because they shrink from the sides of the pan and become firmer, so turning out is easier.
- Use a metal cooling rack for cooling cakes to make sure that any excess steam can escape without making the cake soggy. If you don't have a cooling rack, use the rack from a broiler pan or a barbecue rack.
- Always make sure your cake is completely cool before storing, because if any steam remains, it can cause mold.

GLOSSARY OF BAKING TERMS

BAKING BLIND

Baking a pie shell without filling. Place a round of parchment paper or wax paper in the pie shell and fill with dried beans, rice, or ceramic pie weights, then bake as the recipe instructs.

BEATING

A method of vigorously agitating with a spoon, fork, or electric mixer, to combine ingredients evenly, to soften ingredients, such as butter, or to incorporate air into mixtures.

CREAMING

To beat together mixtures of fat and sugar to soften to a pale, fluffy consistency, incorporating air into the mix to make a light, spongy cake, such as a layer cake.

DREDGING

To sprinkle a mixture or surface generously with a dry ingredient, such as flour or confectioners' sugar, either using a sifter or a dredger, which has a top with holes for even sprinkling.

DUSTING

To sprinkle a surface lightly with a dry ingredient, such as flour, confectioners' sugar, or spices, to give a thin coating, using a fine sifter or dredger to distribute evenly.

FOLDING IN

A method of combining a creamed mixture with dry ingredients, or to incorporate whisked egg whites, so that as little air as possible is knocked out. Ideally, use a large metal spoon to cut and fold the dry ingredients through the mixture, agitating as little as possible to retain air bubbles for lightness.

GLAZING

To brush a coating over a mixture, either before or after baking, to give a glossy appearance or improve the flavor. For instance, beaten egg or milk are used to glaze pastries and breads, and syrups or jams may be brushed over a cake top for an attractive finish.

KNEADING

A process of pressing and stretching a dough, with the hands or a dough hook, to strengthen the gluten (the protein in wheat flour). This makes the gluten more elastic, enabling the dough to rise easily and giving an even texture to the finished product.

PUNCHING DOWN

This is a second kneading, usually done after the dough has been left to rise and before shaping, with the purpose of punching out any large air bubbles from the dough to guarantee an even-textured result.

PIPING

Forcing a soft cake or cookie mixture, or a frosting, from a pastry bag through a tip, usually to create a decorative shape or effect, such as stars, rosettes, or lines. Use a firm, even pressure for best results.

RISING

To let a bread dough to stand after shaping, usually in a warm place. This is done to let the dough rise and give the finished bread a good rise and a light, even texture.

RUBBING IN

A method of incorporating fat, such as butter, into dry ingredients, such as flour, using the fingertips to rub the two together evenly. The fingertips are the coolest part of the hand, and a cool, light touch helps to give a short texture to pie dough, cookies, and cakes.

SIFTING

To shake dry ingredients, such as flour, through a sifter or strainer to eliminate lumps and create a smooth texture. It can also help to evenly distribute any added rising agents or spices.

WHIPPING

A term used to describe the gentle beating of a mixture, usually with a mixer, to make it smooth or incorporate air. For example, it is used to thicken heavy cream, or make it stiff enough for piping.

WHISKING

Rapidly beating a mixture using a hand whisk or electric mixer to incorporate and trap large amounts of air. This method is used for whisked sponge cakes, which rely totally on air for a light, open texture, and meringues, where egg whites are whisked until they are stiff enough to hold peaks.

1

CAKES

Nothing can beat the sight and taste of a freshly baked cake. But cakes shouldn't just be enjoyed on birthdays or special occasions. There is no time like the present to dig out your apron, get baking, and rediscover the joy of an afternoon's cake making. You'll find all the traditional favorites in this chapter as well as some new ideas that make cakes something everyone can enjoy any day of the week.

SPONGE LAYER CAKE

SERVES 8–10

INGREDIENTS
- ¾ CUP UNSALTED BUTTER, AT ROOM TEMPERATURE, PLUS EXTRA FOR GREASING
- ¾ CUP SUPERFINE SUGAR
- 3 EGGS, BEATEN
- SCANT 1½ CUPS SELF-RISING FLOUR
- PINCH OF SALT
- 3 TBSP RASPBERRY JAM
- 1 TBSP SUPERFINE OR CONFECTIONERS' SUGAR

1 Preheat the oven to 350°F/180°C.

2 Grease two 8-inch/20-cm round cake pans and line with wax or parchment paper.

3 Cream the butter and superfine sugar together in a mixing bowl using a wooden spoon or a handheld mixer until the batter is pale in color and light and fluffy.

4 Add the eggs, one at a time, beating well after each addition.

5 Sift the flour and salt together into a separate bowl and carefully add to the batter, folding it in with a metal spoon or a spatula.

6 Divide the batter between the pans and smooth over with a spatula.

7 Place the pans in the center of the oven and bake for 25–30 minutes, until well risen, golden brown, and beginning to shrink from the sides of the pan.

8 Remove from the oven and let stand for 1 minute.

9 Loosen the cakes from around the edge of the pans using a palette knife. Turn the cakes out onto a clean dish towel, remove the paper, and invert the cakes onto a wire rack (this prevents the wire rack from marking the top of the cakes).

10 When completely cool, sandwich together the cakes with the jam and sprinkle with the superfine or confectioners' sugar.

DOUBLE CHOCOLATE MINT SPONGE

SERVES 8

INGREDIENTS
- ¾ CUP UNSALTED BUTTER, SOFTENED, PLUS EXTRA FOR GREASING
- GENEROUS 1¼ CUPS ALL-PURPOSE FLOUR
- 2 TBSP UNSWEETENED COCOA POWDER
- 1 TBSP BAKING POWDER
- SCANT 1 CUP SUPERFINE SUGAR
- 3 EGGS, BEATEN
- 1 TBSP MILK
- 12 CHOCOLATE MINT STICKS, CHOPPED
- ⅔ CUP CHOCOLATE SPREAD, PLUS EXTRA TO DRIZZLE
- CHOCOLATE MINT STICKS TO DECORATE

1 Preheat the oven to 350°F/180°C. Grease and line the bottom of two 8-inch/20-cm layer cake pans.

2 Sift the flour, unsweetened cocoa powder, and baking powder into a bowl and beat in the butter, sugar, and eggs, mixing until smooth. Stir in the milk and chocolate mint pieces.

3 Spread the batter into the pans. Bake for 25–30 minutes, until risen and firm. Cool in the pans for 2 minutes, then turn out and finish cooling on a wire rack.

4 Sandwich the cakes together with chocolate spread, then drizzle more chocolate spread over the top. Decorate the cake with chocolate mint sticks.

CHOCOLATE
FUDGE CAKE

SERVES 8

INGREDIENTS
- ¾ CUP BUTTER, SOFTENED, PLUS EXTRA FOR GREASING
- GENEROUS 1 CUP SUPERFINE SUGAR
- 3 EGGS, BEATEN
- 3 TBSP DARK CORN SYRUP
- 3 TBSP GROUND ALMONDS
- GENEROUS 1 CUP SELF-RISING FLOUR
- PINCH OF SALT
- ¼ CUP UNSWEETENED COCOA

FROSTING
- 8 OZ/225 G SEMISWEET CHOCOLATE, BROKEN INTO PIECES
- ¼ CUP DARK BROWN SUGAR
- 1 CUP BUTTER, DICED
- 5 TBSP EVAPORATED MILK
- ½ TSP VANILLA EXTRACT

1 Grease and line the bottoms of two 8-inch/20-cm round layer cake pans.

2 To make the frosting, place the chocolate, brown sugar, butter, evaporated milk, and vanilla extract in a heavy-bottom pan. Heat gently, stirring continuously, until melted. Pour into a bowl and let cool. Cover and let chill in the refrigerator for 1 hour, or until spreadable.

3 Preheat the oven to 350°F/180°C. Place the butter and superfine sugar in a bowl and beat together until light and fluffy. Gradually beat in the eggs. Stir in the corn syrup and ground almonds. Sift the flour, salt, and cocoa into a separate bowl, then fold into the cake batter. Add a little water, if necessary, to make a dropping consistency.

4 Spoon the cake batter into the prepared pans and bake in the preheated oven for 30–35 minutes, or until springy to the touch and a skewer inserted in the center comes out clean.

5 Let stand in the pans for 5 minutes, then turn out onto wire racks to cool completely. When the cakes have cooled, sandwich them together with half the frosting. Spread the remaining frosting over the top and sides of the cake, swirling it to give a frosted appearance.

COCONUT & LIME CAKE

INGREDIENTS
- ¾ CUP UNSALTED BUTTER, SOFTENED, PLUS EXTRA FOR GREASING
- GENEROUS ¾ CUP SUPERFINE SUGAR
- 3 EGGS, BEATEN
- 1 CUP SELF-RISING FLOUR
- SCANT 1 CUP UNSWEETENED DRIED SHREDDED COCONUT
- GRATED RIND AND JUICE OF 1 LIME

FROSTING
- 1½ CUPS CONFECTIONERS' SUGAR
- GRATED RIND AND JUICE OF 1 LIME
- ¼ CUP UNSWEETENED DRIED SHREDDED COCONUT, LIGHTLY TOASTED

1 Preheat the oven to 325°F/160°C. Grease an 8-inch/20-cm round cake pan and line with parchment paper.

2 Place the butter and sugar in a large bowl and beat together until pale and fluffy. Gradually beat in the eggs. Sift in the flour and gently fold in using a metal spoon. Fold in the coconut and the lime rind and juice.

3 Spoon the batter into the prepared pan and level the surface. Bake in the preheated oven for 1 hour—1 hour 10 minutes, until risen, golden, and firm to the touch. Let cool in the pan for 5 minutes, then turn out and cool completely on a wire rack.

4 For the frosting, sift the confectioner's sugar into a bowl. Stir in the lime rind and juice to make a thick smooth frosting, adding a few drops of water, if necessary. Spoon the frosting over the top of the cake, letting it drizzle down the sides of the cake. Scatter the toasted shredded coconut over the frosting and let set.

CLEMENTINE CAKE

SERVES 8

INGREDIENTS
- ¾ CUP BUTTER, SOFTENED, PLUS EXTRA FOR GREASING
- 2 CLEMENTINES
- ¾ CUP SUPERFINE SUGAR
- 3 EGGS, LIGHTLY BEATEN
- 1¼ CUPS SELF-RISING FLOUR
- 3 TBSP GROUND ALMONDS
- 3 TBSP LIGHT CREAM

GLAZE & TOPPING
- 6 TBSP CLEMENTINE JUICE
- 2 TBSP SUPERFINE SUGAR
- 3 WHITE SUGAR LUMPS, CRUSHED

1 Preheat the oven to 350°F/180°C. Grease a 7-inch/18-cm round pan with butter and line the bottom with baking parchment.

2 Pare the zest from the clementines and chop it finely. In a bowl, cream together the butter, sugar, and clementine zest until pale and fluffy.

3 Gradually add the beaten eggs to the batter, beating thoroughly after each addition.

4 Gently fold in the flour, ground almonds, and light cream. Spoon the batter into the prepared pan.

5 Bake in a preheated oven, for 55–60 minutes, or until a fine skewer inserted into the center comes out clean. Let cool slightly.

6 Meanwhile, make the glaze. Put the clementine juice into a small pan with the superfine sugar. Bring to a boil over a low heat and simmer for 5 minutes.

7 Turn out the cake onto a wire rack. Drizzle the glaze over the cake until it has been absorbed and sprinkle with the crushed sugar lumps. Let cool completely before serving.

CHOCOLATE
GANACHE CAKE

SERVES 10

INGREDIENTS
- ¾ CUP UNSALTED BUTTER, PLUS EXTRA FOR GREASING
- ¾ CUP SUPERFINE SUGAR
- 4 EGGS, LIGHTLY BEATEN
- 1¾ CUPS SELF-RISING FLOUR
- 1 TBSP UNSWEETENED COCOA
- 1¾ OZ/50 G SEMISWEET CHOCOLATE, MELTED
- 7 OZ/200 G CHOCOLATE-FLAVORED CONFECTIONERY COATING, TO DECORATE

GANACHE
- 2 CUPS HEAVY CREAM
- 13 OZ/375 G SEMISWEET CHOCOLATE, BROKEN INTO PIECES

1 Preheat the oven to 350°F/180°C. Lightly grease and line an 8-inch/20-cm springform round cake pan with parchment paper.

2 Beat the butter and sugar together in a bowl until light and fluffy. Gradually add the eggs, beating well after each addition. Sift the flour and cocoa together, then fold into the cake batter. Fold in the melted chocolate.

3 Pour into the prepared pan and smooth the top. Bake in the preheated oven for 40 minutes, or until springy to the touch. Let the cake cool for 5 minutes in the pan, then turn out onto a wire rack and let cool completely. Cut the cooled cake into two layers.

4 To make the ganache, place the cream in a saucepan and bring to a boil, stirring. Add the chocolate and stir until melted. Pour into a bowl, let cool, then chill for 2 hours, or until set and firm. Whisk the mixture until light and fluffy and set aside.

5 Reserve one third of the ganache. Use the remainder to sandwich the cake together and spread over the cake.

6 Melt the confectionery coating and spread it over a large sheet of parchment paper. Let cool until just set. Cut into strips a little wider than the height of the cake. Place the strips around the edge of the cake, overlapping them slightly.

7 Pipe the reserved ganache in teardrops or shells to cover the top of the cake. Let chill for 1 hour before serving.

CLASSIC CHERRY CAKE

SERVES 8

INGREDIENTS
- SCANT 1 CUP BUTTER, PLUS EXTRA FOR GREASING
- GENEROUS 1 CUP CANDIED CHERRIES, QUARTERED
- ¾ CUP GROUND ALMONDS
- 1¾ CUPS ALL-PURPOSE FLOUR
- 1 TSP BAKING POWDER
- 1 CUP SUPERFINE SUGAR
- 3 EXTRA-LARGE EGGS
- FINELY GRATED RIND AND JUICE OF 1 LEMON
- 6 SUGAR CUBES, CRUSHED

1 Preheat the oven to 350°F/180°C. Grease an 8-inch/20-cm round cake pan and line the bottom and sides with nonstick parchment paper.

2 Stir together the candied cherries, ground almonds, and 1 tablespoon of the flour. Sift the remaining flour into a separate bowl with the baking powder.

3 Cream together the butter and sugar until light in color and fluffy in texture. Gradually add the eggs, beating hard with each addition, until evenly mixed.

4 Add the flour mixture and fold lightly and evenly into the creamed mixture with a metal spoon. Add the cherry mixture and fold in evenly. Finally, fold in the lemon rind and juice.

5 Spoon the batter into the prepared cake pan and sprinkle with the crushed sugar cubes. Bake in the preheated oven for 1–1¼ hours, or until risen, golden brown, and the cake is just beginning to shrink away from the sides of the pan.

6 Cool in the pan for about 15 minutes, then turn out to finish cooling on a wire rack.

SPICED APPLE & RAISIN CAKE

SERVES 8–10

INGREDIENTS
- 1 CUP UNSALTED BUTTER, SOFTENED, PLUS EXTRA FOR GREASING
- GENEROUS 1 CUP LIGHT BROWN SUGAR
- 4 LARGE EGGS, LIGHTLY BEATEN
- SCANT 1⅔ CUPS SELF-RISING FLOUR
- 2 TSP GROUND CINNAMON
- ½ TSP GROUND NUTMEG
- ½ CUP GOLDEN RAISINS
- 3 SMALL APPLES, PEELED, CORED, AND THINLY SLICED
- 2 TBSP HONEY, WARMED

1 Preheat the oven to 350°F/180°C. Grease a 9-inch/23-cm round springform cake pan and line the bottom with parchment paper.

2 Place the butter and sugar in a large bowl and beat together until light and fluffy. Gradually beat in the eggs. Sift the flour, cinnamon, and nutmeg into the batter and fold in gently using a metal spoon. Fold in the golden raisins.

3 Spoon half the batter into the prepared pan and level the surface. Scatter over half the sliced apples. Spoon over the rest of the cake mixture and gently level the surface. Arrange the rest of the apple slices over the top.

4 Bake in the preheated oven for 1 hour 10 minutes–1 hour 15 minutes, until risen, golden brown, and firm to the touch. Let cool in the pan for 10 minutes, then turn out onto a cooling rack. Brush the top with the warmed honey and let cool completely.

HUMMINGBIRD
CAKE

SERVES 10

INGREDIENTS
- SCANT 1 CUP SUNFLOWER OIL, PLUS EXTRA FOR GREASING
- 2¼ CUPS ALL-PURPOSE FLOUR
- 1¼ CUPS SUPERFINE SUGAR
- 1 TSP GROUND CINNAMON
- 1 TSP BAKING SODA
- 3 EGGS, BEATEN
- SCANT 1 CUP PECANS, COARSELY CHOPPED, PLUS EXTRA TO DECORATE
- 1 CUP MASHED RIPE BANANAS (ABOUT 3 BANANAS)
- 3 OZ/85 G CANNED CRUSHED PINEAPPLE (DRAINED WEIGHT), PLUS 4 TBSP JUICE FROM THE CAN

FROSTING
- ¾ CUP CREAM CHEESE
- 4 TBSP CUP UNSALTED BUTTER
- 1 TSP VANILLA EXTRACT
- 3½ CUPS CONFECTIONERS' SUGAR

1 Preheat the oven to 350°F/180°C. Lightly grease three 9-inch/23-cm layer cake pans with oil and line the bottoms with parchment paper.

2 Sift together the flour, superfine sugar, cinnamon, and baking soda into a large bowl. Add the eggs, oil, pecans, bananas, and pineapple with the juice and stir with a wooden spoon until evenly mixed.

3 Divide the batter among the prepared pans, spreading it evenly. Bake in the preheated oven for 25–30 minutes, or until golden brown and firm to the touch.

4 Remove the cakes from the oven and let cool for 10 minutes in the pans before turning out onto wire racks to cool.

5 For the frosting, beat together the cream cheese, butter, and vanilla extract in a bowl until smooth. Sift in the confectioners' sugar and mix until smooth.

6 Sandwich the cakes together with half of the frosting, spread the remaining frosting over the top, then sprinkle with pecans to decorate.

COFFEE & WALNUT CAKE

SERVES 8

INGREDIENTS
- ¾ CUP BUTTER, PLUS EXTRA FOR GREASING
- ¾ CUP LIGHT BROWN SUGAR
- 3 EXTRA-LARGE EGGS, BEATEN
- 3 TBSP STRONG BLACK COFFEE
- 1½ CUPS SELF-RISING FLOUR
- 1½ TSP BAKING POWDER
- 1 CUP WALNUT PIECES
- WALNUT HALVES, TO DECORATE

FROSTING
- ½ CUP BUTTER
- 1¾ CUPS CONFECTIONERS' SUGAR
- 1 TBSP STRONG BLACK COFFEE
- ½ TSP VANILLA EXTRACT

1 Preheat the oven to 350°F/180°C. Grease and line the bottoms of two 8-inch/20-cm round layer cake pans.

2 Cream together the butter and brown sugar until pale and fluffy. Gradually add the eggs, beating well after each addition. Beat in the coffee.

3 Sift the flour and baking powder into the batter, then fold in lightly and evenly with a metal spoon. Fold in the walnut pieces.

4 Divide the batter between the prepared cake pans and smooth level. Bake in the preheated oven for 20–25 minutes, or until golden brown and springy to the touch. Turn out onto a wire rack to cool.

5 For the frosting, beat together the butter, confectioners' sugar, coffee, and vanilla extract, mixing until smooth and creamy.

6 Use about half of the frosting to sandwich the cakes together, then spread the remaining frosting on top and swirl with a metal spatula. Decorate with walnut halves.

CHOCOLATE & ALMOND
LAYER CAKE

SERVES 10–12

INGREDIENTS
- 4 TBSP BUTTER, MELTED, PLUS EXTRA FOR GREASING
- 7 EGGS
- 1¾ CUPS SUPERFINE SUGAR
- 1¼ CUPS ALL-PURPOSE FLOUR
- ½ CUP UNSWEETENED COCOA

FILLING
- 7 OZ SEMISWEET DARK CHOCOLATE
- ½ CUP BUTTER
- 4 TBSP CONFECTIONERS' SUGAR

TO DECORATE
- 10 TBSP TOASTED SLIVERED ALMONDS, CRUSHED LIGHTLY
- GRATED CHOCOLATE

1 Preheat the oven to 350°F/180°C. Grease a deep 9-inch/23-cm square cake pan and line the bottom with baking parchment.

2 Whisk the eggs and superfine sugar in a mixing bowl with an electric mixer for about 10 minutes, or until the batter is very light and foamy and the beaters leaves a trail that lasts a few seconds when lifted.

3 Sift the flour and cocoa together and fold half into the batter. Drizzle over the melted butter and fold in the rest of the flour and cocoa. Pour into the prepared pan and bake in a preheated oven for 30–35 minutes, or until springy to the touch. Let cool slightly, then remove from the pan and cool completely on a wire rack.

4 To make the filling, melt the chocolate and butter together, then remove from the heat. Stir in the confectioners' sugar and let cool, then beat until thick enough to spread.

5 Halve the cake lengthwise and cut each half into 3 layers. Sandwich the layers together with three fourths of the chocolate filling. Spread the remainder over the cake and mark a wavy pattern on the top. Press the almonds onto the sides. Decorate with grated chocolate.

CLASSIC CARROT CAKE

SERVES 12

INGREDIENTS
- BUTTER, FOR GREASING
- 1 CUP SELF-RISING FLOUR
- PINCH OF SALT
- 1 TSP GROUND CINNAMON
- ¾ CUP LIGHT BROWN SUGAR
- 2 EGGS
- SCANT ½ CUP SUNFLOWER OIL
- 2 MEDIUM CARROTS, PEELED AND FINELY GRATED
- ⅓ CUP SHREDDED COCONUT
- ⅓ CUP WALNUTS, CHOPPED
- WALNUT PIECES, FOR DECORATING

FROSTING
- 4 TBSP BUTTER, SOFTENED
- 3 TBSP CREAM CHEESE
- 1½ CUPS CONFECTIONERS' SUGAR, SIFTED
- 1 TSP LEMON JUICE

1 Preheat the oven to 350°F/180°C. Lightly grease an 8-inch/20-cm square cake pan and line the bottom with parchment paper.

2 Sift the flour, salt, and ground cinnamon into a large bowl and stir in the brown sugar. Add the eggs and oil to the dry ingredients and mix well.

3 Stir in the grated carrot, shredded coconut, and chopped walnuts.

4 Pour the batter into the prepared pan and bake in the preheated oven for 20–25 minutes, or until just firm to the touch. Let cool in the pan.

5 Meanwhile, make the frosting. In a bowl, beat together the butter, cream cheese, confectioners' sugar, and lemon juice, until the mixture is fluffy and creamy.

6 Turn the cake out of the pan and cut into 12 bars or slices. Spread with the frosting and then decorate with walnut pieces.

BANANA LOAF

SERVES 8

INGREDIENTS
- BUTTER, FOR GREASING
- SCANT 1 CUP WHITE SELF-RISING FLOUR
- SCANT ¾ CUP WHOLE WHEAT SELF-RISING FLOUR
- GENEROUS ¾ CUP RAW BROWN SUGAR
- PINCH OF SALT
- ½ TSP GROUND CINNAMON
- ½ TSP GROUND NUTMEG
- 2 LARGE RIPE BANANAS, PEELED
- ¾ CUP ORANGE JUICE
- 2 EGGS, BEATEN
- 4 TBSP CANOLA OIL

1 Preheat the oven to 350°F/180°C. Lightly grease and line a 9 x 5 x 3-inch/ 23 x 13 x 8-cm loaf pan.

2 Sift the flours, sugar, salt, and the spices into a large bowl. In a separate bowl, mash the bananas with the orange juice, then stir in the eggs and oil. Pour into the dry ingredients and mix well.

3 Spoon into the prepared loaf pan and bake in the preheated oven for 1 hour, then test to see if the loaf is cooked by inserting a skewer into the center. If it comes out clean, the loaf is done. If not, bake for an additional 10 minutes and test again.

4 Remove from the oven and let cool in the pan. Turn out the loaf, slice, and serve.

BUTTERNUT SQUASH & ORANGE CAKE

SERVES 10–12

INGREDIENTS
- ¾ CUP BUTTER, SOFTENED, PLUS EXTRA FOR GREASING
- ¾ CUP LIGHT BROWN SUGAR
- 3 EGGS, BEATEN
- FINELY GRATED RIND AND JUICE OF 1 ORANGE
- 2 CUPS WHOLE WHEAT FLOUR
- 3 TSP BAKING POWDER
- 1 TSP GROUND CINNAMON
- 1⅓ CUPS COARSELY GRATED BUTTERNUT SQUASH
- GENEROUS ¾ CUP GOLDEN RAISINS

TOPPING
- 1 CUP CREAM CHEESE
- ¼ CUP CONFECTIONER'S SUGAR, SIFTED
- 1 TSP FINELY GRATED ORANGE RIND (RESERVED FROM CAKE INGREDIENTS)
- 2–3 TSP FRESHLY SQUEEZED ORANGE JUICE (RESERVED FROM CAKE INGREDIENTS)
- THINLY PARED ORANGE ZEST, TO DECORATE

1 Preheat the oven to 350°F/180°C. Grease and line a deep 7-inch/18-cm round cake pan and set aside. For the cake, cream the butter and sugar together in a bowl until light and fluffy.

2 Gradually beat in the eggs, beating well after each addition. Reserve 1 teaspoon of the orange rind for the topping, then beat the remaining orange rind into the creamed mixture. Fold in the flour, baking powder, and cinnamon, then fold in the squash, golden raisins, and a little orange juice, if necessary (about 1 tablespoon) to create a fairly soft consistency.

3 Turn the batter into the prepared pan and level the surface. Bake for about 1 hour, until risen, firm to the touch, and deep golden brown. Remove from the oven and cool in the pan for a few minutes, then turn out onto a wire rack. Remove the lining paper and let cool completely.

4 To make the topping, beat the cream cheese, confectioner's sugar, reserved grated orange rind, and 2–3 teaspoons of the reserved orange juice together in a bowl until smooth and combined. Spread over the top of the cold cake, swirling it attractively, then sprinkle with pared orange zest. Serve immediately in slices.

LEMON DRIZZLE CAKE

SERVES 8

INGREDIENTS
- BUTTER, FOR GREASING
- 1¾ CUPS ALL-PURPOSE FLOUR
- 2 TSP BAKING POWDER
- 1 CUP SUPERFINE SUGAR
- 4 EGGS
- ⅔ CUP SOUR CREAM
- GRATED RIND OF 1 LARGE LEMON
- 4 TBSP LEMON JUICE
- ⅔ CUP SUNFLOWER OIL

SYRUP
- 4 TBSP CONFECTIONERS' SUGAR
- 3 TBSP LEMON JUICE

1 Preheat the oven to 350°F/180°C. Lightly grease an 8-inch/20-cm loose-bottom round cake pan and line the bottom with parchment paper.

2 Sift the flour and baking powder into a mixing bowl and stir in the superfine sugar.

3 In a separate bowl, whisk the eggs, sour cream, lemon rind, lemon juice, and oil together.

4 Pour the egg mixture into the dry ingredients and mix well until evenly combined.

5 Pour the batter into the prepared pan and bake in the preheated oven for 45–60 minutes, or until risen and golden brown.

6 Meanwhile, to make the syrup, mix together the confectioners' sugar and lemon juice in a small pan. Stir over low heat until just beginning to bubble and turn syrupy.

7 As soon as the cake comes out of the oven, prick the surface with a fine skewer, then brush the syrup over the top. Let the cake cool completely in the pan before turning out and serving.

GINGERBREAD

MAKES 12–16

INGREDIENTS
- 3¾ CUPS ALL-PURPOSE FLOUR
- 1 TBSP BAKING POWDER
- 1 TSP BAKING SODA
- 1 TBSP GROUND GINGER
- ¾ CUP UNSALTED BUTTER
- ¾ CUP BROWN SUGAR
- ¾ CUP BLACKSTRAP MOLASSES
- ¾ CUP MAPLE SYRUP OR CORN SYRUP
- 1 EGG, BEATEN
- 1 CUP MILK
- CREAM OR WARMED MAPLE SYRUP, FOR SERVING

1 Preheat the oven to 325°F/160°C.

2 Line a 9-inch/23-cm square cake pan, 2 inches/5 cm deep, with wax or parchment paper.

3 Sift the flour, baking powder, baking soda, and ground ginger into a large mixing bowl.

4 Place the butter, brown sugar, molasses, and maple syrup in a medium saucepan and heat over low heat until the butter has melted and the sugar has dissolved. Set aside to cool briefly.

5 Mix the beaten egg with the milk and add to the cooled syrup mixture.

6 Add the liquid ingredients to the dry ingredients and beat well using a wooden spoon until the batter is smooth and glossy.

7 Pour the batter into the prepared pan and bake in the center of the oven for 1½ hours, until well risen and just firm to the touch. This makes a lovely sticky gingerbread, but if you like a firmer cake cook, for an additional 15 minutes.

8 Remove from the oven and let the cake to cool in the pan on a wire rack. When cooled, remove the cake from the pan with the wax paper. To store, wrap with foil and place in an airtight container for up to 1 week to let the flavors develop.

9 Cut into wedges and serve as an afternoon snack or with cream for dessert. Drizzling some warmed maple syrup on top is an added extravagance.

WHITE CHOCOLATE
COFFEE GÂTEAU

SERVES 8–10

INGREDIENTS
- 3 TBSP UNSALTED BUTTER, PLUS EXTRA FOR GREASING
- 3 OZ/85 G WHITE CHOCOLATE
- ⅔ CUP SUPERFINE SUGAR
- 4 EXTRA-LARGE EGGS, BEATEN
- 2 TBSP VERY STRONG BLACK COFFEE
- 1 TSP VANILLA EXTRACT
- GENEROUS 1 CUP ALL-PURPOSE FLOUR
- WHITE CHOCOLATE CURLS, TO DECORATE

FROSTING
- 6 OZ/175 G WHITE CHOCOLATE
- 6 TBSP UNSALTED BUTTER
- GENEROUS ½ CUP SOUR CREAM
- GENEROUS 1 CUP CONFECTIONERS' SUGAR, SIFTED
- 1 TBSP COFFEE LIQUEUR OR VERY STRONG BLACK COFFEE

1 Preheat the oven to 350°F/180°C. Grease two 8-inch/20-cm layer cake pans and line the bottoms with parchment paper.

2 Place the butter and chocolate in a bowl set over a saucepan of hot, but not simmering, water and leave on very low heat until just melted. Stir to mix lightly, then remove from the heat.

3 Place the superfine sugar, eggs, coffee, and vanilla extract in a large bowl set over a saucepan of hot water and whisk hard with an electric mixer until the mixture is pale and thick enough to leave a trail when the beaters are lifted.

4 Remove from the heat, sift in the flour, and fold in lightly and evenly. Quickly fold in the butter-and-chocolate mixture, then divide the batter between the prepared pans.

5 Bake in the preheated oven for 25–30 minutes, until risen, golden brown, and springy to the touch. Cool in the pans for 2 minutes, then run a knife around the edges to loosen and turn out onto a wire rack to cool.

6 For the frosting, place the chocolate and butter in a bowl set over a saucepan of hot water and heat gently until melted. Remove from the heat, stir in the sour cream, then add the confectioners' sugar and coffee liqueur and mix until smooth. Chill the frosting for at least 30 minutes, stirring occasionally, until it becomes thick and glossy.

7 Use about one third of the frosting to sandwich the cakes together. Spread the remainder over the top and sides, swirling with a spatula. Arrange the chocolate curls over the top of the cake and let set.

2

SMALL CAKES & BARS

Whether you are catering for a children's party or special occasion, or just want to treat friends and family, small cakes and bars will always hit the spot. With a fabulous selection of cupcakes, muffins, brownies, and bars, all tastes can be catered for with ease. This chapter includes all the favorites as well as several exciting new options that will enchant both children and adults alike.

CARROT & ORANGE CUPCAKES WITH MASCARPONE FROSTING

MAKES 12

INGREDIENTS
- 8 TBSP BUTTER, SOFTENED, OR SOFT MARGARINE
- GENEROUS ½ CUP FIRMLY PACKED BROWN SUGAR
- JUICE AND FINELY GRATED RIND OF 1 SMALL ORANGE
- 2 LARGE EGGS, LIGHTLY BEATEN
- 3 MEDIUM CARROTS, GRATED
- ¼ CUP WALNUT PIECES, COARSELY CHOPPED
- SCANT 1 CUP ALL-PURPOSE FLOUR
- 1 TSP GROUND PUMPKIN PIE SPICE
- 1½ TSP BAKING POWDER

FROSTING
- 1¼ CUPS MASCARPONE CHEESE
- 4 TBSP CONFECTIONERS' SUGAR
- GRATED RIND OF 1 LARGE ORANGE

1 Preheat the oven to 350°F/180°C. Put 12 paper liners in a muffin pan.

2 Put the butter, sugar, and orange rind in a bowl and beat together until light and fluffy. Gradually add the eggs, beating well after each addition. Squeeze any excess liquid from the carrots and add to the batter with the walnuts and orange juice. Stir into the batter until well mixed. Sift in the flour, pumpkin pie spice, and baking powder and then, using a metal spoon, fold into the batter. Spoon the batter into the paper liners.

3 Bake the cupcakes in the preheated oven for 25 minutes, or until well risen, firm to the touch, and golden brown. Transfer to a wire rack and let cool.

4 To make the frosting, put the mascarpone cheese, confectioners' sugar, and orange rind in a large bowl and beat together until well mixed.

5 When the cupcakes are cold, spread the frosting on top of each cupcake, swirling it with a round-bladed knife. Store the cupcakes in the refrigerator until ready to serve.

BLUEBERRY MUFFINS

MAKES 10–12

INGREDIENTS
- 1⅔ CUPS ALL-PURPOSE FLOUR
- 1 TSP BAKING POWDER
- PINCH OF SALT
- ½ CUP RAW BROWN SUGAR, PLUS 1 TBSP FOR SPRINKLING
- 1 EGG, BEATEN
- SCANT 1 CUP MILK
- 4 TBSP UNSALTED BUTTER, MELTED
- 4½ OZ/125 G SMALL FRESH BLUEBERRIES

1 Preheat the oven to 350°F/180°C. Line a 12-hole muffin pan with paper liners. Sift the flour, baking powder, and salt into a large bowl and stir in the sugar.

2 Add the beaten egg, milk, and melted butter to the dry ingredients and stir in lightly until just combined—do not overmix. Carefully fold in the blueberries.

3 Spoon the batter into the paper liners, being careful not to overfill, and sprinkle with the remaining sugar.

4 Bake in the preheated oven for 25–30 minutes, or until golden brown and firm. Transfer to a wire rack to cool a little.

DOUBLE CHOCOLATE MUFFINS

MAKES 12

INGREDIENTS
- SCANT ½ CUP BUTTER, SOFTENED
- SCANT ¾ CUP SUPERFINE SUGAR
- ½ CUP DARK BROWN SUGAR
- 2 EGGS
- ⅔ CUP SOUR CREAM
- 5 TBSP MILK
- 2 CUPS ALL-PURPOSE FLOUR
- 1 TSP BAKING SODA
- 2 TBSP UNSWEETENED COCOA
- 1 CUP SEMISWEET CHOCOLATE CHIPS

1 Preheat the oven to 375°F/190°C. Place 12 muffin paper liners in a muffin pan.

2 Put the butter, superfine sugar, and brown sugar into a bowl and beat well. Beat in the eggs, sour cream, and milk until thoroughly mixed. Sift the flour, baking soda, and cocoa into a separate bowl and stir into the mixture. Add the chocolate chips and mix well.

3 Spoon the batter into the paper liners. Bake in the preheated oven for 25–30 minutes. Remove from the oven and let cool for 10 minutes. Turn out onto a wire rack and let cool completely.

VANILLA FROSTED
CUPCAKES

MAKES 12

INGREDIENTS
- ½ CUP UNSALTED BUTTER, SOFTENED
- GENEROUS ½ CUP SUPERFINE SUGAR
- 2 EGGS, LIGHTLY BEATEN
- ¾ CUP SELF-RISING FLOUR
- 1 TBSP MILK
- CANDIED ROSE PETALS, TO DECORATE

FROSTING
- ¾ CUP UNSALTED BUTTER, SOFTENED
- 2 TSP VANILLA EXTRACT
- 2 TBSP MILK
- SCANT 2⅔ CUPS CONFECTIONERS' SUGAR, SIFTED

1 Preheat the oven to 350°F/180°C. Put 12 paper liners in a 12-hole muffin pan.

2 Place the butter and sugar in a bowl and beat together until light and fluffy. Gradually beat in the eggs. Sift in the flour and fold in gently using a metal spoon. Fold in the milk.

3 Spoon the batter into the paper liners. Bake in the preheated oven for 15–20 minutes, until golden brown and firm to the touch. Transfer to a cooling rack and let cool.

4 To make the frosting, put the butter, vanilla extract, and milk in a large bowl. Using a handheld mixer beat the mixture until smooth. Gradually beat in the confectioners' sugar and continue beating for 2–3 minutes, until the frosting is light and creamy.

5 Spoon the frosting into a large piping bag fitted with a large star nozzle and pipe swirls of the frosting onto the top of each cupcake. Decorate each cupcake with candied rose petals.

DRIZZLED HONEY
CUPCAKES

MAKES 12

INGREDIENTS
- HEAPING ½ CUP SELF-RISING WHITE FLOUR
- ¼ TSP GROUND CINNAMON
- PINCH OF GROUND CLOVES
- PINCH OF GRATED NUTMEG
- 6 TBSP BUTTER, SOFTENED
- SCANT ½ CUP SUPERFINE SUGAR
- 1 TBSP HONEY
- FINELY GRATED RIND OF 1 ORANGE
- 2 EGGS, LIGHTLY BEATEN
- ¾ CUP WALNUT PIECES, FINELY CHOPPED

TOPPING
- 2 TBSP WALNUT PIECES, MINCED
- ¼ TSP GROUND CINNAMON
- 2 TBSP HONEY
- JUICE OF 1 ORANGE

1 Preheat the oven to 375°F/190°C. Put 12 paper liners in a muffin pan, or put 12 double-layer paper liners on a baking sheet.

2 Sift the flour, cinnamon, cloves, and nutmeg together into a bowl. Put the butter and sugar in a separate bowl and beat together until light and fluffy. Beat in the honey and orange rind, then gradually add the eggs, beating well after each addition. Using a metal spoon, fold in the flour mixture. Stir in the walnuts, then spoon the batter into the paper liners.

3 Bake the cupcakes in the preheated oven for 20 minutes, or until well risen and golden brown. Transfer to a wire rack and let cool.

4 To make the topping, mix together the walnuts and cinnamon. Put the honey and orange juice in a pan and heat gently, stirring, until combined.

5 When the cupcakes have almost cooled, prick the tops all over with a fork or skewer and then drizzle with the warm honey mixture. Sprinkle the walnut mixture over the top of each cupcake and serve warm or cold.

DATE, PISTACHIO
& HONEY SLICES

MAKES 12 SLICES

INGREDIENTS
- 1½ CUPS CHOPPED, PITTED DRIED DATES
- 2 TBSP LEMON JUICE
- 2 TBSP WATER
- ¾ CUP PISTACHIO NUTS, CHOPPED
- 2 TBSP HONEY
- MILK, TO GLAZE

PASTRY
- 2 CUPS ALL-PURPOSE FLOUR
- 2 TBSP SUPERFINE SUGAR
- ⅔ CUP BUTTER
- 4–5 TBSP COLD WATER, TO MIX

1 Preheat the oven to 400°F/200°C. Put the dates, lemon juice, and water in a pan and bring to a boil, stirring. Remove from the heat.

2 Stir in the pistachios and 1 tablespoon honey and let cool.

3 For the pastry dough, put the flour, sugar, and butter in a food processor and process to fine crumbs.

4 Mix in just enough cold water to bind to a soft, nonsticky dough.

5 Roll out the dough on a floured surface to two 12 x 8 inch/30 x 20 cm rectangles. Place one on a baking sheet.

6 Spread the date-and-nut mixture to within ½ inch/1 cm of the edge. Top with the remaining dough.

7 Press to seal, trim the edges, and mark into 12 slices. Glaze with milk.

8 Bake in the oven for 20–25 minutes, brush with the remaining honey, and cool on a wire rack.

9 Cut into slices and serve at coffee time or as a lunchtime snack.

CHOCOLATE CHIP
BROWNIES

MAKES 12

INGREDIENTS
- 1 CUP BUTTER, SOFTENED, PLUS EXTRA FOR GREASING
- 5½ OZ/150 G SEMISWEET CHOCOLATE, BROKEN INTO PIECES
- HEAPING 1½ CUPS SELF-RISING FLOUR
- SCANT ⅔ CUP SUPERFINE SUGAR
- 4 EGGS, BEATEN
- ⅔ CUP SHELLED PISTACHIOS, CHOPPED
- 3½ OZ/100 G WHITE CHOCOLATE, COARSELY CHOPPED
- CONFECTIONERS' SUGAR, FOR DUSTING

1 Preheat the oven to 350°F/180°C. Grease a 9-inch/23-cm square baking pan and line with parchment paper.

2 Place the chocolate and softened butter in a heatproof bowl set over a pan of simmering water. Stir until melted, then let cool slightly.

3 Sift the flour into a separate bowl and stir in the superfine sugar.

4 Stir the beaten eggs into the chocolate mixture, then pour the mixture into the flour and sugar and beat well. Stir in the pistachios and white chocolate, then pour the batter into the pan, using a spatula to spread it evenly.

5 Bake in the preheated oven for 30–35 minutes, or until firm to the touch around the edges. Let cool in the pan for 20 minutes. Turn out onto a wire rack. Dust with confectioners' sugar and let cool completely. Cut into 12 pieces and serve.

MAKES 15

INGREDIENTS
- 1 CUP BUTTER, SOFTENED, PLUS EXTRA FOR GREASING
- GENEROUS 1½ CUPS SELF-RISING FLOUR
- 1 TSP BAKING POWDER
- 1 TSP UNSWEETENED COCOA, PLUS EXTRA FOR DUSTING
- GENEROUS 1 CUP SUPERFINE SUGAR
- 4 EGGS, BEATEN
- 3 TBSP INSTANT COFFEE POWDER, DISSOLVED IN 2 TBSP HOT WATER

WHITE CHOCOLATE FROSTING
- 4 OZ/115 G WHITE CHOCOLATE, BROKEN INTO PIECES
- 4 TBSP BUTTER, SOFTENED
- 3 TBSP MILK
- 1¾ CUPS CONFECTIONERS' SUGAR

CAPPUCCINO BROWNIES

1 Grease an 11 x 7-inch/28 x 18-cm shallow cake pan and line the bottom with parchment paper.

2 Sift the flour, baking powder, and cocoa into a bowl and add the butter, superfine sugar, eggs, and coffee. Beat well, by hand or with an electric mixer, until smooth, then spoon into the prepared pan and smooth the top.

3 Bake in the preheated oven for 35–40 minutes, or until risen and firm. Let cool in the pan for 10 minutes, then turn out onto a wire rack and peel off the lining paper. Let cool completely.

4 To make the frosting, place the chocolate, butter, and milk in a bowl set over a saucepan of gently simmering water and stir until the chocolate has melted. Remove the bowl from the pan and sift in the confectioners' sugar. Beat until smooth, then spread over the cake. Dust the top of the cake with cocoa, then cut into squares.

MALTED CHOCOLATE BARS

MAKES 16

INGREDIENTS
- 6 TBSP BUTTER, PLUS EXTRA FOR GREASING
- 2 TBSP CORN SYRUP
- 2 TBSP MALTED CHOCOLATE DRINK
- 8 OZ/225 G MALTED MILK COOKIES
- 2¾ OZ/75 G LIGHT OR SEMISWEET CHOCOLATE, BROKEN INTO PIECES
- 2 TBSP CONFECTIONERS' SUGAR
- 2 TBSP MILK

1 Grease and line the bottom of a shallow 7-inch/18-cm round cake pan or tart pan.

2 Place the butter, corn syrup, and malted chocolate drink in a small pan and heat gently, stirring all the time until the butter has melted and the mixture is well combined.

3 Crush the cookies in a plastic bag with a rolling pin, or process them in a food processor. Stir the cookie crumbs into the chocolate mixture and mix well.

4 Press the mixture into the prepared pan and then chill in the refrigerator until firm.

5 Place the chocolate pieces in a small heatproof bowl with the sugar and the milk. Place the bowl over a pan of gently simmering water and stir until the chocolate melts and the mixture is combined.

6 Spread the chocolate frosting over the cookie base and let the frosting set in the pan. Using a sharp knife, cut into bars to serve.

ROCK CAKES

MAKES 8–10

INGREDIENTS
- ½ CUP BUTTER, PLUS EXTRA FOR GREASING
- 2 CUPS ALL-PURPOSE FLOUR
- 2 TSP BAKING POWDER
- ⅓ CUP LIGHT BROWN SUGAR
- ⅓ CUP MIXED DRIED FRUIT
- FINELY GRATED RIND OF 1 LEMON
- 1 EGG
- 1–2 TBSP MILK
- 2 TSP RAW BROWN SUGAR

1 Preheat the oven to 400°F/200°C. Lightly grease two cookie sheets.

2 Sift the flour and baking powder into a large bowl and rub in the butter using your fingertips until it resembles fine breadcrumbs. Stir in the light brown sugar, mixed dried fruit, and lemon rind.

3 Beat the egg lightly with a tablespoon of the milk and stir into the flour mixture, adding a little more milk if necessary, until it starts to bind together to form a moist but firm dough.

4 Spoon small heaps of the batter on the prepared cookie sheets. Sprinkle with the raw brown sugar.

5 Bake in the preheated oven for 15–20 minutes, or until golden brown and firm. Use a metal spatula to transfer the cakes onto a wire rack to cool.

NUTTY GRANOLA BARS

MAKES 16

INGREDIENTS
- ½ CUP BUTTER, PLUS EXTRA FOR GREASING
- SCANT 2¾ CUPS ROLLED OATS
- ¾ CUP CHOPPED HAZELNUTS
- 6 TBSP ALL-PURPOSE FLOUR
- 2 TBSP CORN SYRUP
- SCANT ½ CUP BROWN SUGAR

1 Preheat the oven to 350°F/180°C, then grease a 9-inch/23-cm square ovenproof dish or cake pan. Place the rolled oats, chopped hazelnuts, and flour in a large mixing bowl and stir together.

2 Place the butter, corn syrup, and sugar in a pan over low heat and stir until melted. Pour onto the dry ingredients and mix well. Turn into the prepared ovenproof dish and smooth the surface with the back of a spoon.

3 Bake in the oven for 20–25 minutes, or until golden and firm to the touch. Mark into 16 pieces and let cool in the dish. When completely cooled, cut through with a sharp knife and remove from the dish.

CHOCOLATE
PEANUT BUTTER
SQUARES

MAKES 20

INGREDIENTS
- 10½ OZ/300 G MILK CHOCOLATE
- 2½ CUPS ALL-PURPOSE FLOUR
- 1 TSP BAKING POWDER
- 1 CUP BUTTER
- 1¾ CUPS LIGHT BROWN SUGAR
- 2 CUPS ROLLED OATS
- ½ CUP CHOPPED MIXED NUTS
- 1 EGG, BEATEN
- 14 OZ/400 G CANNED SWEETENED CONDENSED MILK
- ⅓ CUP CRUNCHY PEANUT BUTTER

1 Preheat the oven to 350°F/180°C. Finely chop the chocolate. Sift the flour and baking powder into a large bowl. Add the butter to the flour mixture and rub in using your fingertips until the mixture resembles breadcrumbs. Stir in the sugar, rolled oats, and chopped nuts.

2 Put a quarter of the mixture into a bowl and stir in the chocolate. Set aside.

3 Stir the egg into the remaining mixture, then press into the bottom of a 12 x 8-inch/30 x 20-cm cake pan. Bake in the preheated oven for 15 minutes.

4 Meanwhile, mix the condensed milk and peanut butter together. Pour into the cake pan and spread evenly, then sprinkle the reserved chocolate mixture on top and press down lightly.

5 Return to the oven and bake for an additional 20 minutes, until golden brown. Let cool in the pan, then cut into squares.

CHOCOLATE & APRICOT SQUARES

MAKES 12

INGREDIENTS
- 9 TBSP BUTTER, PLUS EXTRA FOR GREASING
- 6 OZ/175 G WHITE CHOCOLATE, CHOPPED
- 4 EGGS
- ½ CUP SUPERFINE SUGAR
- 1¾ CUPS ALL-PURPOSE FLOUR, SIFTED
- 1 TSP BAKING POWDER
- PINCH OF SALT
- ½ CUP PLUMPED DRIED APRICOTS, CHOPPED

1 Preheat the oven to 350°F/180°C. Lightly grease a 20-cm/8-inch square cake pan and line the bottom with a sheet of parchment paper.

2 Melt the butter and chocolate in a heatproof bowl set over a pan of gently simmering water. Stir frequently with a wooden spoon until the mixture is smooth and glossy. Let the mixture cool slightly.

3 Beat the eggs and superfine sugar into the butter-and-chocolate mixture until well combined.

4 Fold in the flour, baking powder, salt, and chopped dried apricots and mix thoroughly.

5 Pour the mixture into the pan and bake in the preheated oven for about 25–30 minutes.

6 The center of the cake may not be completely firm, but it will set as it cools. Leave in the pan to cool.

7 When the cake is completely cold, turn it out carefully and slice into bars or small squares.

VIENNESE JAM SHORTCAKES

MAKES 12

INGREDIENTS
- 1 CUP UNSALTED BUTTER, SOFTENED
- 1 TSP VANILLA EXTRACT
- ¾ CUP CONFECTIONERS' SUGAR
- 1¼ CUPS SELF-RISING FLOUR
- GENEROUS ⅓ CUP CORNSTARCH
- 2 TBSP STRAWBERRY JAM
- CONFECTIONERS' SUGAR, TO DUST

1 Preheat the oven to 350°F/180°C. Put 12 paper liners in a 12-hole muffin pan.

2 Place the butter and vanilla extract in a large bowl and using an electric handheld mixer beat together until the butter is very soft. Sift in the confectioners' sugar and beat thoroughly.

3 Sift together the flour and cornstarch and stir into the mixture until smooth. Spoon the mixture into a large piping bag fitted with a large star nozzle and pipe swirls of the mixture into the paper liners, leaving a slight dip in the center of each one.

4 Bake in the preheated oven for 15–20 minutes, until golden. Let the shortcakes cool in the pan for 15 minutes, then transfer to a cooling rack and let cool completely.

5 Spoon a little jam into the center of each shortcake and dust with confectioners' sugar.

LEMON DRIZZLE
BARS

MAKES 12

INGREDIENTS
- ⅔ CUP SOFT MARGARINE, PLUS EXTRA FOR GREASING
- 2 EGGS
- GENEROUS ¾ CUP SUPERFINE SUGAR
- FINELY GRATED RIND OF 1 LEMON
- 1½ CUPS SELF-RISING FLOUR
- ½ CUP MILK
- CONFECTIONERS' SUGAR, FOR DUSTING

SYRUP
- 1¼ CUPS CONFECTIONERS' SUGAR
- ¼ CUP FRESH LEMON JUICE

1 Preheat the oven to 350°F/180°C. Grease a 7-inch/ 18-cm square cake pan and line with nonstick parchment paper.

2 Place the eggs, superfine sugar, and margarine in a bowl and beat hard until smooth and fluffy. Stir in the lemon rind, then fold in the flour lightly and evenly. Stir in the milk, mixing evenly, then spoon into the prepared cake pan, smoothing level.

3 Bake in the preheated oven for 45–50 minutes, or until golden brown and firm to the touch. Remove from the oven and place the pan on a wire rack.

4 To make the syrup, place the confectioners' sugar and lemon juice in a small saucepan and heat gently, stirring until the sugar dissolves. Do not boil.

5 Prick the warm cake all over with a skewer and spoon the hot syrup evenly over the top.

6 Let cool completely in the pan, then turn out the cake, cut into 12 pieces, and dust with a little confectioners' sugar before serving.

HAZELNUT BARS

MAKES 16

INGREDIENTS
- ⅓ CUP BUTTER, CUT INTO SMALL PIECES, PLUS EXTRA FOR GREASING
- 1¼ CUPS ALL-PURPOSE FLOUR
- PINCH OF SALT
- 1 TSP BAKING POWDER
- 1 CUP SOFT BROWN SUGAR
- 1 EGG, BEATEN
- 4 TBSP MILK
- 1 CUP HAZELNUTS, HALVED
- BROWN CRYSTAL SUGAR, FOR SPRINKLING (OPTIONAL)

1 Preheat the oven to 350°F/180°C. Grease a 9-inch/23-cm square cake pan and line the bottom with baking parchment.

2 Sift the flour, salt, and baking powder into a large mixing bowl.

3 Rub in the butter with your fingers until the mixture resembles fine breadcrumbs. Stir in the brown sugar.

4 Add the egg, milk, and nuts to the mixture and stir well until thoroughly combined.

5 Spoon the mixture into the prepared cake pan and level the surface. Sprinkle with brown sugar, if using.

6 Bake in a preheated oven for about 25 minutes, or until the mixture is firm to the touch when pressed with a finger.

7 Let cool for 10 minutes, then loosen the edges with a round-bladed knife and turn out onto a wire rack. Cut into squares.

CHOCOLATE CARAMEL SHORTBREAD

MAKES 12

INGREDIENTS
- ½ CUP BUTTER, PLUS EXTRA FOR GREASING
- GENEROUS 1 CUP ALL-PURPOSE FLOUR
- GENEROUS ¼ CUP SUPERFINE SUGAR

FILLING & TOPPING
- ¾ CUP BUTTER
- GENEROUS ½ CUP SUPERFINE SUGAR
- 3 TBSP DARK CORN SYRUP
- 14 OZ/400 G CANNED SWEETENED CONDENSED MILK
- 7 OZ/200 G SEMISWEET CHOCOLATE, BROKEN INTO PIECES

1 Preheat the oven to 350°F/180°C. Grease a 9-inch/23-cm shallow square cake pan and line the bottom with parchment paper.

2 Place the butter, flour, and sugar in a food processor and process until it starts to bind together. Press into the prepared pan and level the top. Bake in the preheated oven for 20–25 minutes, or until golden.

3 Meanwhile, make the caramel filling. Place the butter, sugar, corn syrup, and condensed milk in a heavy-bottom saucepan. Heat gently until the sugar has dissolved. Bring to a boil, then reduce the heat and let simmer for 6–8 minutes, stirring, until very thick. Pour over the shortbread and let chill in the refrigerator for 2 hours, or until firm.

4 Place the chocolate in a heatproof bowl set over a saucepan of gently simmering water and stir until melted. Let cool slightly, then spread over the caramel. Let chill in the refrigerator for 2 hours, or until set. Cut the shortbread into 12 pieces using a sharp knife and serve.

3

COOKIES

No coffee break or afternoon snack would be complete without a selection of homemade cookies alongside. Turn your mid-morning break or afternoon treat into something extra special with some of the tantalizing recipes in this chapter. The possibilities for inventiveness when baking cookies are endless and guarantee that you will always be coming back for more.

CHOCOLATE CHIP
COOKIES

MAKES 18

INGREDIENTS
- ½ CUP SOFT MARGARINE, PLUS EXTRA FOR GREASING
- 1½ CUPS ALL-PURPOSE FLOUR, SIFTED
- 1 TSP BAKING POWDER
- SCANT ⅔ CUP LIGHT BROWN SUGAR
- ¼ CUP SUPERFINE SUGAR
- ½ TSP VANILLA EXTRACT
- 1 EGG
- ⅔ CUP SEMISWEET CHOCOLATE CHIPS

1 Preheat the oven to 375°F/190°C. Lightly grease two cookie sheets.

2 Place all the ingredients in a large mixing bowl and beat until they are thoroughly combined.

3 Place tablespoonfuls of the mixture onto the cookie sheets, spacing them well apart to leave room for spreading during cooking.

4 Bake in the oven for 10–12 minutes, until the cookies are golden brown.

5 Using a spatula, transfer the cookies to a cooling rack to cool completely before serving.

CLASSIC OATMEAL COOKIES

MAKES 30

INGREDIENTS
- ¾ CUP BUTTER OR MARGARINE, PLUS EXTRA FOR GREASING
- SCANT 1⅓ CUPS RAW BROWN SUGAR
- 1 EGG
- 4 TBSP WATER
- 1 TSP VANILLA EXTRACT
- 4⅓ CUPS ROLLED OATS
- 1 CUP ALL-PURPOSE FLOUR
- 1 TSP SALT
- ½ TSP BAKING SODA

1 Preheat the oven to 350°F/180°C and grease a large cookie sheet.

2 Cream the butter and sugar together in a large mixing bowl. Beat in the egg, water, and vanilla extract until the mixture is smooth.

3 In a separate bowl, mix the oats, flour, salt, and baking soda together. Gradually stir the oat mixture into the butter mixture until thoroughly combined.

4 Put tablespoonfuls of the mixture onto the prepared cookie sheet, making sure they are well spaced. Transfer to the preheated oven and bake for 15 minutes, or until the cookies are golden brown.

5 Remove the cookies from the oven and place on a wire rack to cool before serving.

PEANUT BUTTER
COOKIES

MAKES 26

INGREDIENTS
- ½ CUP BUTTER, SOFTENED, PLUS EXTRA FOR GREASING
- SCANT ½ CUP CRUNCHY PEANUT BUTTER
- GENEROUS ½ CUP SUPERFINE SUGAR
- GENEROUS ½ CUP LIGHT BROWN SUGAR
- 1 EGG, BEATEN
- ½ TSP VANILLA EXTRACT
- ⅔ CUP ALL-PURPOSE FLOUR
- ½ TSP BAKING SODA
- ½ TSP BAKING POWDER
- PINCH OF SALT
- 1½ CUPS ROLLED OATS

1 Preheat the oven to 350°F/180°C, then grease three cookie sheets.

2 Place the butter and peanut butter in a bowl and beat together. Beat in the superfine sugar and brown sugar, then gradually beat in the egg and vanilla extract.

3 Sift the flour, baking soda, baking powder, and salt into the bowl and stir in the oats.

4 Place spoonfuls of the cookie dough onto the cookie sheets, spaced well apart to leave room for spreading. Flatten slightly with a fork.

5 Bake in the preheated oven for 12 minutes, or until lightly browned. Let cool on the cookie sheets for 2 minutes, then transfer to wire racks to cool completely.

CHOCOLATE CHIP & CINNAMON COOKIES

MAKES ABOUT 30

INGREDIENTS
- 1 CUP BUTTER, SOFTENED
- SCANT ¾ CUP SUPERFINE SUGAR
- 1 EGG YOLK, LIGHTLY BEATEN
- 2 TSP ORANGE EXTRACT
- 2½ CUPS ALL-PURPOSE FLOUR
- PINCH OF SALT
- GENEROUS ½ CUP SEMISWEET CHOCOLATE CHIPS

CINNAMON COATING
- 1½ TBSP SUPERFINE SUGAR
- 1½ TBSP GROUND CINNAMON

1 Preheat the oven to 375°F/190°C. Line 2 cookie sheets with baking parchment.

2 Put the butter and sugar into a bowl and mix well with a wooden spoon, then beat in the egg yolk and orange extract. Sift together the flour and a pinch of salt into the mixture, add the chocolate chips, and stir until thoroughly combined.

3 For the coating, mix together the sugar and cinnamon in a shallow dish. Scoop out tablespoons of the cookie dough, roll them into balls, then roll them in the cinnamon mixture to coat. Put them on the prepared cookie sheets spaced well apart.

4 Bake for 12–15 minutes. Let cool on the cookie sheets for 5–10 minutes, then using a metal spatula, carefully transfer to wire racks to cool completely.

FROSTED ORANGE
COOKIES

MAKES ABOUT 30

INGREDIENTS
- ⅓ CUP BUTTER, SOFTENED
- ⅓ CUP SUPERFINE SUGAR
- 1 EGG
- 1 TBSP MILK
- 2 CUPS ALL-PURPOSE FLOUR
- ¼ CUP UNSWEETENED COCOA

FROSTING
- 1 CUP CONFECTIONERS'
  SUGAR, SIFTED
- 3 TBSP ORANGE JUICE
- A LITTLE DARK CHOCOLATE,
  MELTED

1 Preheat the oven to 350°F/180°C. Carefully line 2 cookie sheets with baking parchment.

2 Beat together the butter and sugar until light and fluffy. Beat in the egg and milk until well combined. Sift together the flour and unsweetened cocoa and gradually mix together to form a soft dough. Use your fingers to incorporate the last of the flour and to bring the dough together.

3 Roll out the dough onto a lightly floured counter until ⅛ inch/5 mm thick. Using a 2-inch/5-cm fluted round cutter, cut out as many cookies as you can. Reroll the dough trimmings and cut out more cookies.

4 Place the cookies on the prepared cookie sheets and bake in a preheated oven for 10–12 minutes, or until golden.

5 Let the cookies cool on the cookie sheets for a few minutes, then transfer to a wire rack to cool completely.

6 To make the frosting, place the confectioners' sugar in a bowl and stir in enough orange juice to form a thin icing that will coat the back of a spoon. Spread the frosting over the cookies and let it set. Drizzle with melted chocolate. Let the chocolate set before serving.

CHOCOLATE SPREAD & HAZELNUT DROPS

MAKES ABOUT 30

INGREDIENTS
- 1 CUP BUTTER, SOFTENED
- SCANT ¾ CUP SUPERFINE SUGAR
- 1 EGG YOLK, LIGHTLY BEATEN
- 2 TSP VANILLA EXTRACT
- 2 CUPS ALL-PURPOSE FLOUR
- ½ CUP UNSWEETENED COCOA POWDER
- PINCH OF SALT
- ½ CUP GROUND HAZELNUTS
- ⅓ CUP SEMISWEET CHOCOLATE CHIPS
- 4 TBSP CHOCOLATE AND HAZELNUT SPREAD

1 Preheat the oven to 375°F/190°C. Line 2 cookie sheets with parchment paper.

2 Put the butter and sugar into a bowl and mix well with a wooden spoon, then beat in the egg yolk and vanilla extract. Sift together the flour, unsweetened cocoa, and a pinch of salt into the mixture, add the ground hazelnuts and chocolate chips, and stir until thoroughly combined.

3 Scoop out tablespoons of the mixture and shape into balls with your hands, then put them on the prepared cookie sheets spaced well apart. Use the dampened handle of a wooden spoon to make a hollow in the center of each cookie.

4 Bake for 12–15 minutes. Let cool on the cookie sheets for 5–10 minutes, then using a metal spatula, carefully transfer the cookies to wire racks to cool completely. When they have cooled down completely, fill the hollows in the center with chocolate and hazelnut spread.

PECAN & MAPLE COOKIES

MAKES 18

INGREDIENTS
- ½ CUP BUTTER, SOFTENED, PLUS EXTRA FOR GREASING
- ½ CUP PECAN NUTS
- 2 TBSP MAPLE SYRUP
- SCANT ½ CUP LIGHT BROWN SUGAR
- 1 LARGE EGG YOLK, LIGHTLY BEATEN
- GENEROUS ¾ CUP SELF-RISING FLOUR

1 Preheat the oven to 375°F/190°C. Lightly grease 2 cookie sheets. Reserve 18 pecan halves and roughly chop the rest.

2 Place the butter, maple syrup, and sugar in a bowl and beat together with a wooden spoon until light and fluffy. Beat in the egg yolk. Sift over the flour and add the chopped pecan nuts. Mix to a stiff dough.

3 Place 18 golf ball-size spoonfuls of the mixture onto the cookie sheets, spaced well apart. Top each with a reserved pecan nut, pressing down gently.

4 Bake in the preheated oven for 10–12 minutes, until light golden brown. Let the cookies cool on the cookie sheets for 10 minutes, then transfer to a cooling rack and let cool completely.

COCONUT & CRANBERRY
COOKIES

MAKES ABOUT 30

INGREDIENTS
- 1 CUP BUTTER, SOFTENED
- SCANT ¾ CUP SUPERFINE SUGAR
- 1 EGG YOLK, LIGHTLY BEATEN
- 2 TSP VANILLA EXTRACT
- 2½ CUPS ALL-PURPOSE FLOUR
- PINCH OF SALT
- ½ CUP UNSWEETENED DRIED COCONUT
- ½ CUP DRIED CRANBERRIES

1 Preheat the oven to 375°F/190°C. Line 2 cookie sheets with parchment paper.

2 Put the butter and sugar into a bowl and mix well with a wooden spoon, then beat in the egg yolk and vanilla extract. Sift together the flour and a pinch of salt into the mixture, add the coconut and cranberries, and stir until thoroughly combined. Scoop up tablespoons of the dough and place in mounds on the prepared cookie sheets spaced well apart.

3 Bake for 12–15 minutes, until golden brown. Let cool on the cookie sheets for 5–10 minutes, then using a metal spatula, carefully transfer to wire racks to cool completely.

GINGERSNAPS

MAKES 30

INGREDIENTS
- ½ CUP BUTTER, PLUS EXTRA FOR GREASING
- 2½ CUPS SELF-RISING FLOUR
- PINCH OF SALT
- 1 CUP SUPERFINE SUGAR
- 1 TBSP GROUND GINGER
- 1 TSP BAKING SODA
- ¼ CUP DARK CORN SYRUP
- 1 EGG, LIGHTLY BEATEN
- 1 TSP GRATED ORANGE RIND

1 Preheat the oven to 325°F/160°C. Lightly grease several cookie sheets.

2 Sift together the flour, salt, sugar, ground ginger, and baking soda into a large mixing bowl.

3 Heat the butter and corn syrup together in a saucepan over very low heat until the butter has melted.

4 Let the butter mixture cool slightly, then pour it onto the dry ingredients. Add the egg and orange rind and mix together thoroughly.

5 Using your hands, carefully shape the dough into 30 even-size balls. Place the balls on the prepared cookie sheets, spaced well apart, then flatten them slightly with your fingers.

6 Bake in the preheated oven for 15–20 minutes. Carefully transfer the cookies to a wire rack to cool and crisp.

FLORENTINE COOKIES

MAKES 18

INGREDIENTS
- ½ CUP BUTTER, SOFTENED, PLUS EXTRA FOR GREASING
- GENEROUS ½ CUP SUPERFINE SUGAR
- 1 EGG, BEATEN
- 1¼ CUPS ALL-PURPOSE FLOUR
- ½ TSP BAKING SODA
- ¼ CUP SLIVERED ALMONDS, LIGHTLY CRUSHED
- ¼ CUP CANDIED CHERRIES, CHOPPED
- 1 CUP MIXED PEEL
- ⅓ CUP GOLDEN RAISINS
- 3 OZ/85 G SEMISWEET DARK CHOCOLATE, MELTED

1 Preheat the oven to 375°F/190°C. Lightly grease 2 cookie sheets.

2 Place the butter and sugar in a bowl and beat together until pale and fluffy. Beat in the egg. Sift in the flour and baking soda and mix to a soft dough.

3 Mix together the almonds, cherries, mixed peel, and golden raisins. Stir half into the cookie dough. Place 18 heaped spoonfuls of the dough onto the cookie sheets, spaced well apart. Sprinkle with the rest of the fruit-and-nut mixture.

4 Bake in the preheated oven for 10–12 minutes, until pale golden. Let the cookies cool on the cookie sheets for 10 minutes, then transfer to a cooling rack and let cool completely.

5 Use a teaspoon to drizzle melted chocolate over each cookie. Let set.

SPICED RUM COOKIES

MAKES 18

INGREDIENTS
- ¾ CUP UNSALTED BUTTER, PLUS EXTRA FOR GREASING
- 1 CUP DARK BROWN SUGAR
- 2 CUPS ALL-PURPOSE FLOUR
- PINCH OF SALT
- ½ TSP BAKING SODA
- 1 TSP GROUND CINNAMON
- ½ TSP GROUND CORIANDER
- ½ TSP GROUND NUTMEG
- ¼ TSP GROUND CLOVES
- 2 TBSP DARK RUM

1 Preheat the oven to 350°F/180°C. Lightly grease 2 cookie sheets.

2 Cream together the butter and sugar and whisk until light and fluffy.

3 Sift the flour, salt, baking soda, cinnamon, coriander, nutmeg, and cloves into the creamed mixture.

4 Pour the dark rum into the creamed mixture and stir well.

5 Using 2 teaspoons, place small mounds of the mixture, onto the cookie sheets, placing them 3 inches/7.5 cm apart leaving room for spreading during cooking. Flatten each one slightly with the back of a spoon.

6 Bake in a preheated oven for 10–12 minutes, or until golden.

7 Let the cookies cool and become crisp on wire racks before serving.

WALNUT & COFFEE COOKIES

MAKES ABOUT 30

INGREDIENTS
- 2 ENVELOPES INSTANT LATTE
- 1 TBSP HOT WATER
- 1 CUP BUTTER, SOFTENED
- SCANT ¾ CUP SUPERFINE SUGAR
- 1 EGG YOLK, LIGHTLY BEATEN
- 2½ CUPS ALL-PURPOSE FLOUR
- PINCH OF SALT
- SCANT 1 CUP FINELY CHOPPED WALNUTS
- COFFEE SUGAR CRYSTALS, FOR SPRINKLING

1 Put the instant latte into a bowl and stir in the hot, but not boiling water to make a paste. Put the butter and sugar into a bowl and mix well with a wooden spoon, then beat in the egg yolk and coffee paste. Sift together the flour and a pinch of salt into the mixture, add the walnuts, and stir until thoroughly combined. Halve the dough, shape into balls, wrap in plastic wrap, and chill in the refrigerator for 30–60 minutes.

2 Preheat the oven to 375°F/190°C. Line 2 cookie sheets with parchment paper.

3 Unwrap the dough and roll out between 2 sheets of parchment paper to about ⅛ inch/3 mm thick. Stamp out cookies with a 2½-inch/6-cm round cutter and put them on the prepared cookie sheets spaced well apart.

4 Lightly brush the cookies with water, sprinkle with the coffee sugar crystals, and bake for 10–12 minutes. Let cool on the cookie sheets for 5–10 minutes, then using a metal spatula, carefully transfer the cookies to wire racks to cool completely.

OATY RAISIN & HAZELNUT COOKIES

MAKES ABOUT 30

INGREDIENTS
- SCANT ½ CUP RAISINS, CHOPPED
- ½ CUP ORANGE JUICE
- 1 CUP BUTTER, SOFTENED
- SCANT ¾ CUP SUPERFINE SUGAR
- 1 EGG YOLK, LIGHTLY BEATEN
- 2 TSP VANILLA EXTRACT
- 2 CUPS ALL-PURPOSE FLOUR
- PINCH OF SALT
- ½ CUP ROLLED OATS
- ½ CUP CHOPPED HAZELNUTS
- WHOLE HAZELNUTS, TO DECORATE

1 Preheat the oven to 375°F/190°C. Line 2 cookie sheets with parchment paper. Put the raisins in a bowl, add the orange juice, and let soak for 10 minutes.

2 Put the butter and sugar into a bowl and mix well with a wooden spoon, then beat in the egg yolk and vanilla extract. Sift together the flour and a pinch of salt into the mixture and add the oats and chopped hazelnuts. Drain the raisins, add them to the mixture, and stir until thoroughly combined.

3 Scoop up tablespoons of the mixture and put them in mounds on the prepared cookie sheets spaced well apart. Flatten slightly and place a whole hazelnut in the center of each cookie.

4 Bake for 12–15 minutes, until golden brown. Let cool on the cookie sheets for 5–10 minutes, then using a metal spatula, carefully transfer the cookies to wire racks to cool completely.

LEMON CHOCOLATE PINWHEELS

MAKES 40

INGREDIENTS
- ¾ CUP BUTTER, SOFTENED, PLUS EXTRA FOR GREASING
- 3 CUPS ALL-PURPOSE FLOUR, PLUS EXTRA FOR DUSTING
- 1⅓ CUPS SUPERFINE SUGAR
- 1 EGG, BEATEN
- 1 OZ/25 G SEMISWEET CHOCOLATE, BROKEN INTO PIECES
- GRATED RIND OF 1 LEMON

1 Grease and flour several cookie sheets.

2 In a large mixing bowl, cream together the butter and sugar until light and fluffy.

3 Gradually add the beaten egg to the creamed mixture, beating well after each addition.

4 Sift the flour into the creamed mixture and mix thoroughly until a soft dough forms.

5 Transfer half of the dough to another bowl. Put the chocolate in a heatproof bowl set over a pan of gently simmering water until melted. Cool slightly. Beat in the chocolate.

6 Stir the grated lemon rind into the other half of the plain dough.

7 On a lightly floured work counter, roll out the dough to form 2 rectangles.

8 Lay the lemon dough on top of the chocolate dough. Roll up tightly, using a sheet of parchment paper to guide you. Chill the dough for 1 hour.

9 Preheat the oven to 375°F/190°C. Cut the roll into 40 slices, place them on the cookie sheets, and bake in the oven for 10–12 minutes, or until lightly golden. Transfer the pinwheels to a wire rack and let cool completely before serving.

TURKISH DELIGHT COOKIES

MAKES ABOUT 30

INGREDIENTS
- 1 CUP BUTTER, SOFTENED
- SCANT ¾ CUP ROSE PETAL-FLAVORED SUPERFINE SUGAR
- 1 EGG YOLK, LIGHTLY BEATEN
- 1 TSP ALMOND EXTRACT
- 2½ CUPS ALL-PURPOSE FLOUR
- PINCH OF SALT
- SCANT 1 CUP CHOPPED PISTACHIOS
- 1½ CUPS PINK MINI MARSHMALLOWS, HALVED HORIZONTALLY
- ⅓–⅔ CUP UNSWEETENED DRIED COCONUT

1 Put the butter and sugar into a bowl and mix well with a wooden spoon, then beat in the egg yolk and almond extract. Sift together the flour and a pinch of salt into the mixture, add the pistachios, and stir until thoroughly combined. Halve the dough, shape into balls, wrap in plastic wrap, and chill for 30–60 minutes.

2 Preheat the oven to 375°F/190°C. Line 2 cookie sheets with parchment paper.

3 Unwrap the dough and roll out between 2 sheets of parchment paper. Stamp out 2½-inch/6-cm squares and put them on the prepared cookie sheets.

4 Bake for 12–15 minutes, until light golden brown, then remove from the oven. Cover the tops of the cookies with halved mini marshmallows. Brush with water and sprinkle with the coconut. Return to the oven for about 30 seconds, until the marshmallows have softened. Let cool on the cookie sheets for 5–10 minutes, then using a metal spatula transfer the cookies to wire racks to cool completely.

CHOCOLATE & ORANGE
SANDWICH COOKIES

MAKES ABOUT 15

INGREDIENTS
- 1 CUP BUTTER, SOFTENED
- SCANT ¾ CUP SUPERFINE SUGAR
- 2 TSP FINELY GRATED ORANGE RIND
- 1 EGG YOLK, LIGHTLY BEATEN
- 2 TSP VANILLA EXTRACT
- 2¼ CUPS ALL-PURPOSE FLOUR
- PINCH OF SALT
- ¼ CUP UNSWEETENED COCOA POWDER
- 3½ OZ/100 G SEMISWEET CHOCOLATE, FINELY CHOPPED

CHOCOLATE FILLING
- ½ CUP HEAVY CREAM
- 7 OZ/200 G WHITE CHOCOLATE, BROKEN INTO PIECES
- 1 TSP ORANGE EXTRACT

1 Preheat the oven to 375°F/190°C. Line 2 cookie sheets with parchment paper.

2 Put the butter, sugar, and orange rind into a bowl and mix well with a wooden spoon, then beat in the egg yolk and vanilla extract. Sift together the flour, unsweetened cocoa powder, and a pinch of salt into the mixture, add the chopped chocolate, and stir until thoroughly combined.

3 Scoop up tablespoons of the dough, roll into balls, and put on the prepared cookie sheets spaced well apart. Gently flatten and smooth the tops with the back of a spoon.

4 Bake for 10–15 minutes, until light golden brown. Let cool on the cookie sheets for 5–10 minutes, then using a metal spatula, carefully transfer to wire racks to cool completely.

5 To make the filling, bring the cream to a boil in a small saucepan, then remove the saucepan from the heat. Stir in the chocolate until the mixture is smooth, then stir in the orange extract. When the mixture is completely cool, use to sandwich the cookies together in pairs.

CRUNCHY NUT & HONEY
SANDWICH COOKIES

MAKES ABOUT 30

INGREDIENTS
- 1 CUP BUTTER, SOFTENED
- SCANT ¾ CUP SUPERFINE SUGAR
- 1 EGG YOLK, LIGHTLY BEATEN
- 2 TSP VANILLA EXTRACT
- 2½ CUPS ALL-PURPOSE FLOUR
- PINCH OF SALT
- ⅓ CUP MACADAMIA NUTS, CASHEW NUTS, OR PINE NUTS, CHOPPED

FILLING
- ⅓ CUP BUTTER, SOFTENED
- ¾ CUP CONFECTIONERS' SUGAR
- ⅓ CUP CLOVER OR OTHER SET HONEY

1 Preheat the oven to 375°F/190°C. Line 2 cookie sheets with parchment paper.

2 Put the butter and superfine sugar into a bowl and mix well with a wooden spoon, then beat in the egg yolk and vanilla extract. Sift together the flour and a pinch of salt into the mixture and stir until thoroughly combined.

3 Scoop up tablespoons of the dough and roll into balls. Put half of them on a prepared cookie sheet spaced well apart and flatten gently. Spread out the nuts in a shallow dish and dip one side of the remaining dough balls into them, then place on the other cookie sheet, nut side uppermost, and flatten gently.

4 Bake for 10–15 minutes, until light golden brown. Let cool on the cookie sheets for 5–10 minutes, then using a metal spatula, carefully transfer to wire racks to cool completely.

5 Beat the butter with the confectioners' sugar and honey until creamy and thoroughly mixed. Spread the honey mixture over the plain cookies and top with the nut-coated cookies.

4

SWEET PIES & PASTRIES

In this chapter you will find an abundance of family favorites and comfort foods as well as some tempting new ideas. The delicious aroma of apples as they bake in the oven, and the sheer naughtiness of a gooey chocolate filling will make these recipes hard to resist. Even the most inexperienced cook will have no trouble rustling up something magical.

LEMON MERINGUE PIE

SERVES 4

INGREDIENTS
PIE DOUGH
- HEAPING 1 CUP ALL-PURPOSE FLOUR, PLUS EXTRA FOR DUSTING
- 6 TBSP BUTTER, CUT INTO SMALL PIECES, PLUS EXTRA FOR GREASING
- ¼ CUP CONFECTIONERS' SUGAR, SIFTED
- FINELY GRATED RIND OF ½ LEMON
- ½ EGG YOLK, BEATEN
- 1½ TBSP MILK

- **FILLING**
- 3 TBSP CORNSTARCH
- 1¼ CUPS WATER
- JUICE AND GRATED RIND OF 2 LEMONS
- HEAPING ¾ CUP SUPERFINE SUGAR
- 2 EGGS, SEPARATED

1 To make the pie dough, sift the flour into a bowl. Rub in the butter with your fingertips until the mixture resembles fine breadcrumbs. Mix in the remaining ingredients. Knead briefly on a lightly floured counter. Let rest for 30 minutes.

2 Preheat the oven to 350°F/180°C. Grease an 8-inch/20-cm pie plate with butter. Roll out the pie dough to a thickness of ¼ inch/5 mm; use it to line the bottom and sides of the dish. Prick all over with a fork, line with parchment paper, and fill with dried beans. Bake blind in the oven for 15 minutes. Remove from the oven and take out the paper and beans. Reduce the temperature to 300°F/150°C.

3 To make the filling, mix the cornstarch with a little of the water. Place the remaining water in a pan. Stir in the lemon juice and rind and cornstarch paste. Bring to a boil, stirring.

4 Cook for 2 minutes. Let cool a little. Stir in 5 tablespoons of the sugar and the egg yolks and pour into the pastry shell.

5 Whisk the egg whites in a clean, greasefree bowl until stiff. Whisk in the remaining sugar and spread over the pie. Bake for another 40 minutes. Remove from the oven, cool, and serve.

APPLE PIE

SERVES 6–8

INGREDIENTS
PIE DOUGH
- 2 CUPS ALL-PURPOSE FLOUR
- PINCH OF SALT
- 6 TBSP BUTTER OR MARGARINE, CUT INTO SMALL PIECES
- 6 TBSP LARD OR VEGETABLE SHORTENING, CUT INTO SMALL PIECES
- ABOUT 6 TBSP COLD WATER
- BEATEN EGG OR MILK, FOR GLAZING

- **FILLING**
- 1 LB 10 OZ–2 LB 4 OZ/ 750 G–1 KG BAKING APPLES, PEELED, CORED, AND SLICED
- SCANT ⅔ CUP LIGHT BROWN SUGAR OR SUPERFINE SUGAR, PLUS EXTRA FOR SPRINKLING
- ½–1 TSP GROUND CINNAMON, ALLSPICE, OR GROUND GINGER
- 1–2 TBSP WATER (OPTIONAL)

1 To make the pie dough, sift the flour and salt into a large bowl. Add the butter and lard and rub in using your fingertips until the mixture resembles fine breadcrumbs. Add the water and gather the mixture together into a dough. Wrap the dough and let chill in the refrigerator for 30 minutes.

2 Preheat the oven to 425°F/220°C. Roll out almost two thirds of the pie dough thinly and use to line a deep 9-inch/23-cm pie plate.

3 Mix the apples with the sugar and spice and pack into the pastry shell; the filling can come up above the rim. Add the water if needed, particularly if the apples are a dry variety.

4 Roll out the remaining pie dough to form a lid. Dampen the edges of the pie rim with water and position the lid, pressing the edges firmly together. Trim and crimp the edges.

5 Use the trimmings to cut out leaves or other shapes to decorate the top of the pie. Dampen and attach. Glaze the top of the pie with beaten egg or milk, make one or two slits in the top, and place the pie on a baking sheet.

6 Bake in the preheated oven for 20 minutes, then reduce the temperature to 350°F/180°C and bake for an additional 30 minutes, or until the pastry is a light golden brown. Serve hot or cold, sprinkled with sugar.

Parámetro

SWEET PUMPKIN PIE

SERVES 4

INGREDIENTS
FILLING
- 4 LB/1.8 KG SWEET PUMPKIN
- 1¾ CUPS SWEETENED CONDENSED MILK
- 2 EGGS
- 1 TSP SALT
- ½ TSP VANILLA EXTRACT
- 1 TBSP RAW SUGAR

PIE DOUGH
- 4 TBSP COLD UNSALTED BUTTER, DICED, PLUS EXTRA FOR GREASING
- 1 CUP ALL-PURPOSE FLOUR, PLUS EXTRA FOR DUSTING
- ¼ TSP BAKING POWDER
- 1½ TSP GROUND CINNAMON
- ¾ TSP GROUND NUTMEG
- ¾ TSP GROUND CLOVES
- ¼ CUP SUPERFINE SUGAR
- 1 EGG

TOPPING
- 2 TBSP ALL-PURPOSE FLOUR
- 4 TBSP RAW SUGAR
- 1 TSP GROUND CINNAMON
- 2 TBSP COLD UNSALTED BUTTER, DICED
- HEAPING ⅔ CUP SHELLED PECANS, CHOPPED
- HEAPING ⅔ CUP SHELLED WALNUTS, CHOPPED

1 Preheat the oven to 375°F/190°C. Quarter the pumpkin, remove the seeds, and discard the stem and stringy insides. Place the pumpkin quarters, face down, in a roasting pan and cover with foil. Bake in the oven for 1½ hours, then remove from the oven and let cool. Scoop out the flesh and puree in a food processor. Drain away any excess liquid and chill until ready to use.

2 To make the pie dough, grease a 9-inch/23-cm round pie plate with butter. Sift the flour and baking powder into a bowl. Stir in the spices and the superfine sugar. Rub in the butter until the mixture resembles fine breadcrumbs, then make a well in the center. Beat 1 egg and pour it into the well. Mix together, then use your hands to shape into a ball. Place on a counter, dusted with flour, and roll out to a circle large enough to line the pie plate. Line the plate and trim the edge. Cover the pie plate with plastic wrap and let chill for 30 minutes.

3 Preheat the oven to 425°F/220°C. To make the filling, place the pumpkin puree in a large bowl, then stir in the condensed milk and the 2 eggs. Add the salt, then stir in the vanilla extract and raw sugar. Pour into the pastry shell and bake in the oven for 15 minutes.

4 Meanwhile, make the topping. Combine the flour, sugar, and cinnamon in a bowl, rub in the butter until crumbly, then stir in the nuts. Remove the pie from the oven and reduce the heat to 350°F/180°C. Sprinkle the topping over the pie, then bake for an additional 35 minutes. Remove from the oven and serve hot or cold.

CRISPY CHOCOLATE PIE

SERVES 6

INGREDIENTS
PIE DOUGH
- BUTTER, FOR GREASING
- 2 EGG WHITES
- HEAPING 1 CUP GROUND ALMONDS
- 4 TBSP GROUND RICE
- ⅔ CUP SUPERFINE SUGAR
- ¼ TSP ALMOND EXTRACT

FILLING
- 225 G/8 OZ SEMISWEET DARK CHOCOLATE, BROKEN INTO SMALL PIECES
- 4 EGG YOLKS
- 4 TBSP CONFECTIONERS' SUGAR
- 4 TBSP WHISKEY
- 4 TBSP HEAVY CREAM
- ⅔ CUP WHIPPED CREAM
- 55 G/2 OZ SEMISWEET DARK CHOCOLATE, GRATED, TO DECORATE

1 Preheat the oven to 325°F/160°C. Grease an 8-inch/20-cm tart pan and line the bottom with parchment paper. Whisk the egg whites in a clean, greasefree bowl until stiff peaks form. Gently fold in the ground almonds, ground rice, superfine sugar and almo nd extract. Spread the mixture over the bottom and sides of the prepared pan. Bake in the preheated oven for 15 minutes.

2 Meanwhile, to make the filling, place the chocolate in a heatproof bowl set over a saucepan of barely simmering water until melted. Remove from the heat and let cool slightly, then beat in the egg yolks, confectioners' sugar, whiskey and heavy cream until thoroughly incorporated.

3 Remove the tart pan from the oven and pour in the chocolate mixture. Cover with foil, return to the oven, and bake at the same temperature for 20–25 minutes, until set. Remove from the oven and let to cool completely.

4 Cut the pie into 6 slices. Decorate each slice with whipped cream and grated chocolate. Serve immediately.

MISSISSIPPI MUD PIE

SERVES 12–14

INGREDIENTS
PIE CRUST
- 5 OZ/140 G GRAHAM CRACKERS
- ¾ CUP FINELY CHOPPED PECANS
- 1 TBSP LIGHT BROWN SUGAR
- ½ TSP GROUND CINNAMON
- 6 TBSP BUTTER, MELTED

FILLING
- 1 CUP BUTTER OR MARGARINE, PLUS EXTRA FOR GREASING
- 6 OZ/175 G BITTERSWEET DARK CHOCOLATE
- ½ CUP DARK CORN SYRUP
- 4 LARGE EGGS, BEATEN
- ¾ CUP FINELY CHOPPED PECANS

1 Preheat the oven to 350°F/180°C. Lightly grease a 9-inch/23-cm springform or loose-bottom cake pan.

2 To make the crumb crust, put the graham crackers, pecans, sugar, and cinnamon into a food processor and process until fine crumbs form—do not overprocess to a powder. Add the melted butter and process again until moistened.

3 Tip the crumb mixture into the cake pan and press over the bottom and about 1½ inches/4 cm up the sides of the pan. Cover the pan and chill while making the filling.

4 To make the filling, put the butter, chocolate, and corn syrup into a saucepan over a low heat and stir until melted and blended. Let cool, then beat in the eggs and pecans.

5 Pour the filling into the chilled crumb crust and smooth the surface. Bake in the oven for 30 minutes, or until just set but still soft in the center. Let cool on a wire rack. Serve at room temperature or chilled.

LATTICED CHERRY PIE

SERVES 8

INGREDIENTS
PIE DOUGH
- 1 CUP ALL-PURPOSE FLOUR, PLUS EXTRA FOR DUSTING
- ¼ TSP BAKING POWDER
- ½ TSP ALLSPICE
- ½ TSP SALT
- ¼ CUP SUGAR
- 6 TBSP COLD UNSALTED BUTTER, DICED, PLUS EXTRA FOR GREASING
- 1 BEATEN EGG, PLUS EXTRA FOR GLAZING
- WATER, FOR SEALING

FILLING
- 2 LB/900 G PITTED FRESH OR CANNED CHERRIES, DRAINED
- ¾ CUP SUGAR
- ½ TSP ALMOND EXTRACT
- 2 TSP CHERRY BRANDY
- ¼ TSP ALLSPICE
- 2 TBSP CORNSTARCH
- 2 TBSP WATER

- FRESHLY WHIPPED CREAM OR ICE CREAM, FOR SERVING

1 To make the pie dough, sift the flour and baking powder into a large bowl. Stir in the allspice, salt, and sugar. Using your fingertips, rub in 4 tablespoons of butter until the mixture resembles fine breadcrumbs, then make a well in the center. Pour the beaten egg into the well. Mix with a wooden spoon, then shape the mixture into a dough. Cut the dough in half and use your hands to roll each half into a ball. Wrap the dough in plastic wrap and let chill for 30 minutes.

2 Preheat the oven to 425°F/220°C. Grease a 9-inch/23-cm round pie plate with butter. Roll out the dough into 2 circles, each 12 inches/30 cm in diameter. Use one to line the pie plate. Trim the edges, leaving an overhang of ½ inch/1 cm.

3 To make the filling, place half the cherries and all the sugar in a large pan. Bring to a simmer over low heat, stirring, for 5 minutes, or until the sugar has melted. Stir in the almond extract, brandy, and allspice. In a separate bowl, mix the cornstarch and water to form a paste. Remove the pan from the heat, stir in the cornstarch, then return to the heat and stir constantly until the mixture boils and thickens. Let cool a little. Stir in the remaining cherries, pour into the pastry shell, then dot with the remaining butter.

4 Cut the dough circle into long strips ½ inch/1 cm wide. Lay 5 strips evenly across the top of the filling in the same direction, folding back every other strip. Now lay 6 strips crosswise over the strips, folding back every other strip each time you add another crosswise strip, to form a lattice. Trim off the ends and seal the edges with water. Use your fingers to crimp around the rim, then brush the top with beaten egg. Cover with foil, then bake for 30 minutes. Remove from the oven, discard the foil, then return the pie to the oven for an additional 15 minutes, or until cooked and golden. Serve warm with freshly whipped cream or ice cream.

PECAN PIE

SERVES 8

INGREDIENTS
PIE DOUGH
- 1¾ CUPS ALL-PURPOSE FLOUR, PLUS EXTRA FOR DUSTING
- ½ CUP BUTTER
- 2 TBSP SUPERFINE SUGAR
- A LITTLE COLD WATER

FILLING
- 5 TBSP BUTTER
- SCANT ½ CUP LIGHT BROWN SUGAR
- ⅔ CUP DARK CORN SYRUP
- 2 EXTRA-LARGE EGGS, BEATEN
- 1 TSP VANILLA EXTRACT
- 1 CUP PECANS

1 For the pie dough, place the flour in a bowl and rub in the butter using your fingertips until it resembles fine breadcrumbs. Stir in the superfine sugar and add enough cold water to mix to a firm dough. Wrap in plastic wrap and chill for 15 minutes, until firm enough to roll out.

2 Preheat the oven to 400°F/200°C. Roll out the dough on a lightly floured counter and use to line a 9-inch/23-cm loose-bottom round tart pan. Prick the bottom with a fork. Chill for 15 minutes.

3 Place the tart pan on a cookie sheet and line with a sheet of parchment paper and dried beans. Bake blind in the preheated oven for 10 minutes. Remove the paper and beans and bake for an additional 5 minutes. Reduce the oven temperature to 350°F/180°C.

4 For the filling, place the butter, brown sugar, and corn syrup in a saucepan and heat gently until melted. Remove from the heat and quickly beat in the eggs and vanilla extract.

5 Coarsely chop the pecans and stir into the mixture. Pour into the tart shell and bake for 35–40 minutes, until the filling is just set. Serve warm or cold.

CRANBERRY & ALMOND TART

SERVES 8–10

INGREDIENTS
PIE DOUGH
- ¼ CUPS ALL-PURPOSE FLOUR
- ½ CUP SUPERFINE SUGAR
- ½ CUP BUTTER, CUT INTO SMALL PIECES
- 1 TBSP WATER

FILLING
- 1 CUP UNSALTED BUTTER
- 1 CUP SUPERFINE SUGAR
- 1 EGG
- 2 EGG YOLKS
- 6 TBSP ALL-PURPOSE FLOUR, SIFTED
- 1⅔ CUPS GROUND ALMONDS
- 4 TBSP HEAVY CREAM
- 14½ OZ/410 G CANNED APRICOT HALVES, DRAINED
- 4½ OZ/125 G FRESH CRANBERRIES

1 To make the pastry, place the flour and sugar in a bowl and rub in the butter with your fingers. Add the water and work the mixture together until a soft pastry has formed. Wrap in plastic wrap and let chill for 30 minutes.

2 On a lightly floured counter, roll out the dough and line a 9½-inch/24-cm loose-bottom tart pan. Prick the pastry with a fork and let chill for 30 minutes.

3 Line the pie shell with parchment paper and dried beans and bake blind in a preheated oven, 375°F/190°C, for 15 minutes. Remove the paper and dried beans and cook for an additional 10 minutes.

4 To make the filling, cream together the butter and sugar until light and fluffy. Beat in the egg and egg yolks, then stir in the flour, almonds, and cream.

5 Place the apricot halves and cranberries on the bottom of the pie shell and spoon the filling over the top.

6 Bake in the oven for about 1 hour, or until the topping is just set. Let cool slightly, then serve warm or cold.

COCONUT TART

SERVES 8

INGREDIENTS
PIE DOUGH
- 9 INCH/23-CM PRECOOKED TART SHELL

FILLING
- 2 EGGS
- GRATED RIND AND LIME OF 2 LEMONS
- 1 CUP GOLDEN SUPERFINE SUGAR
- 1¾ CUPS HEAVY CREAM
- 1 CUP DRY UNSWEETENED COCONUT

1 Preheat the oven to 350°F/180°C. To make the filling, put the eggs, lemon rind, and sugar in a bowl and beat together for 1 minute.

2 Gently stir in the cream, then the lemon juice and, finally, the coconut.

3 Spread the mixture into the pastry shell and bake in the oven for 40 minutes, until set and golden. Let cool for about 1 hour to firm up. Serve at room temperature.

PLUM CRUMBLE TART

SERVES 8–10

INGREDIENTS
PIE DOUGH
- 1½ CUPS ALL-PURPOSE FLOUR
- 1 TBSP CORNSTARCH
- ½ TSP BAKING POWDER
- 7 TBSP BUTTER
- ⅓ CUP FINELY CHOPPED HAZELNUTS
- SCANT ¼ CUP SUPERFINE SUGAR
- 2–3 TBSP MILK

FILLING
- 14 OZ/400 G RIPE RED PLUMS
- 1 TBSP CORNSTARCH
- 3 TBSP SUPERFINE SUGAR
- FINELY GRATED RIND OF 1 SMALL ORANGE

- CRÈME FRAÎCHE OR GREEK-STYLE YOGURT, TO SERVE

1 Preheat the oven to 350°F/180°C and preheat a cookie sheet.

2 Sift the flour, cornstarch, and baking powder into a large bowl and rub in the butter using your fingertips until it resembles fine breadcrumbs. Stir in the hazelnuts and sugar with just enough milk to bind together.

3 Remove about a quarter of the mixture, cover, and place in the refrigerator. Gently knead the remainder together and press into the bottom and sides of an 8-inch/20-cm loose-bottom round tart pan.

4 For the filling, halve and pit the plums, cut into quarters, and toss with the cornstarch, sugar, and orange rind. Arrange the plums over the dough.

5 Remove the reserved dough from the refrigerator and, using your fingertips, crumble it over the plums.

6 Place the tart on the cookie sheet and bake in the preheated oven for 40–45 minutes, until lightly browned and bubbling. Serve warm or cold with crème fraîche or Greek-style yogurt.

LEMON & PASSION FRUIT TART

SERVES 8

INGREDIENTS
PASTRY
- SCANT 1½ CUPS ALL-PURPOSE FLOUR
- PINCH OF SALT
- ½ CUP UNSALTED BUTTER, CHILLED AND DICED
- ¼ CUP CONFECTIONERS' SUGAR
- 1 EGG YOLK BLENDED WITH 2 TBSP ICE-COLD WATER

FILLING
- 4 PASSION FRUIT
- JUICE AND FINELY GRATED RIND OF 1 LEMON
- ⅔ CUP HEAVY CREAM
- 4 TBSP CRÈME FRAICHE OR SOUR CREAM
- SCANT ½ CUP SUPERFINE SUGAR
- 2 EGGS PLUS 2 EGG YOLKS

TO SERVE
- CONFECTIONERS' SUGAR TO DUST
- CRÈME FRAÎCHE OR WHIPPED CREAM
- SEEDS AND PULP FROM 1 PASSION FRUIT

1 For the pastry, sift the flour and salt into a bowl. Rub in the butter until the mixture resembles fine breadcrumbs. Stir in the confectioners' sugar and blended egg yolk and mix to a dough. Turn onto a floured surface and knead lightly until smooth. Wrap in plastic wrap and chill for 20 minutes.

2 Preheat the oven to 400°F/200°C and preheat a baking sheet. Roll out the pastry on a lightly floured surface and use to line a fluted 9-inch/23-cm loose-bottom, tart pan. Chill for 20 minutes.

3 Prick the pastry bottom all over with a fork, line with parchment paper, and fill with dried beans. Bake blind on the preheated baking sheet in the oven for 10 minutes. Remove the paper and beans and return the pastry shell to the oven for another 5 minutes, until light golden. Reduce the oven temperature to 350°F/180°C.

4 For the filling, halve the passion fruit and scoop out the seeds and flesh into a fine-holed strainer set over a pitcher. Press with the back of a spoon until you have about ¼ cup of juice in the pitcher.

5 In a large bowl, whisk together the passion fruit juice, lemon juice and rind, cream, crème fraiche, sugar, eggs, and egg yolks until smooth. Pour into the pastry shell.

6 Bake for 30–35 minutes, until the filling has just set. Let cool completely. Serve the tart sliced and dusted with confectioners' sugar, with a spoonful of crème fraîche and some passion fruit seeds and pulp.

PEAR & PECAN STRUDEL

SERVES 4

INGREDIENTS
- 2 RIPE PEARS
- 4 TBSP BUTTER
- 1 CUP FRESH WHITE BREADCRUMBS
- HEAPING ⅓ CUP SHELLED PECANS, CHOPPED
- HEAPING 2 TBSP LIGHT BROWN SUGAR
- FINELY GRATED RIND OF 1 ORANGE
- 3½ OZ/100 G FILO PASTRY, THAWED IF FROZEN
- 6 TBSP ORANGE BLOSSOM HONEY
- 2 TBSP ORANGE JUICE
- SIFTED CONFECTIONERS SUGAR, FOR DUSTING
- STRAINED PLAIN YOGURT, FOR SERVING (OPTIONAL)

1 Preheat the oven to 400°F/200°C. Peel, core, and chop the pears. Melt 1 tablespoon of the butter in a skillet and gently sauté the breadcrumbs until golden. Transfer the breadcrumbs to a bowl and add the pears, nuts, light brown sugar, and orange rind. Place the remaining butter in a small pan and heat until melted.

2 Set aside 1 sheet of filo pastry, keeping it well wrapped, and brush the remaining filo sheets with a little melted butter. Spoon some of the nut filling onto the first filo sheet, leaving a 1-inch/2.5-cm margin around the edge. Build up the strudel by placing more buttered filo sheets on top of the first, spreading each one with nut filling as you build up the layers. Drizzle the honey and orange juice over the top.

3 Fold the short ends over the filling, then roll up, starting at a long side. Carefully lift onto a baking sheet, with the seam facing up. Brush with any remaining melted butter and crumple the reserved sheet of filo pastry around the strudel. Bake for 25 minutes, or until golden and crisp. Dust with sifted confectioners' sugar and serve warm with strained plain yogurt, if using.

APPLE STRUDEL WITH
CIDER SAUCE

SERVES 2–4

INGREDIENTS
- 8 APPLES
- 1 TBSP LEMON JUICE
- ⅔ CUP GOLDEN RAISINS
- 1 TSP GROUND CINNAMON
- ½ TSP GROUND NUTMEG
- 1 TBSP LIGHT BROWN SUGAR
- 6 SHEETS FILO DOUGH, THAWED IF FROZEN
- VEGETABLE OIL SPRAY
- CONFECTIONERS' SUGAR, TO SERVE

SAUCE
- 1 TBSP CORNSTARCH
- 2 CUPS HARD CIDER

1 Preheat the oven to 375°F/190°C. Line a baking sheet with parchment paper.

2 Peel and core the apples and chop them into ½-inch/1-cm dice. Toss the apples in a bowl with the lemon juice, golden raisins, cinnamon, nutmeg, and brown sugar.

3 Lay out a sheet of filo dough, spray with vegetable oil, and lay a second sheet on top. Repeat with a third sheet. Spread over half the apple mixture and roll up lengthwise, tucking in the ends to enclose the filling. Repeat to make a second strudel. Slide onto the baking sheet, spray with oil, and bake in the preheated oven for 15–20 minutes.

4 To make the sauce, blend the cornstarch in a saucepan with a little hard cider until smooth. Add the remaining cider and heat gently, stirring, until the mixture boils and thickens. Serve the strudel warm or cold, dredged with confectioners' sugar and accompanied by the cider sauce.

CREAM PALMIERS

MAKES 8

INGREDIENTS
- ¼ CUP GRANULATED SUGAR
- 8 OZ/225 G PUFF PASTRY
- ⅔ CUP HEAVY CREAM
- 1 TBSP CONFECTIONERS'
  SUGAR, SIFTED
- FEW DROPS VANILLA EXTRACT
- 2 TBSP STRAWBERRY JAM

1 Preheat the oven to 425°F/220°C. Dust the counter with half the sugar and roll out the pastry on the sugared surface to a 10 x 12-inch/25 x 30-cm rectangle.

2 Sprinkle the rest of the sugar over the pastry and gently roll over it with the rolling pin. Roll the two short sides of the pastry into the center until they meet, moisten the edges that meet with a little water, and press together gently. Cut across the roll into 16 even-size slices.

3 Place the slices, cut-side down, on a dampened baking sheet. Use a rolling pin to flatten each one slightly.

4 Bake in the preheated oven for 15–18 minutes, until crisp and golden brown, turning the palmiers over halfway through cooking so that both sides caramelize. Transfer to a wire rack to cool.

5 Whip the cream, confectioners' sugar, and vanilla extract together until softly peaking. Sandwich the palmiers together with the jam and whipped cream and serve within 2–3 hours of filling.

CHOCOLATE PARFAIT SANDWICHES

SERVES 4

INGREDIENTS
- 3 LARGE EGG WHITES
- ¾ CUP SUPERFINE SUGAR
- 5 OZ/140 G WHITE CHOCOLATE, GRATED
- 1¾ CUPS CREAM, WHIPPED
- 12 OZ/350 G PUFF PASTRY
- MELTED CHOCOLATE, TO DRIZZLE

1 To make the parfait, beat the egg whites and the sugar together in a heatproof bowl, then set the bowl over a pan of gently simmering water. Using an electric mixer, beat the whites over the heat until you have a light and fluffy meringue. This will take up to 10 minutes. Remove from the heat, add the chocolate, and keep whisking to cool. Fold in the whipping cream.

2 Spoon the parfait into a shallow, rectangular freezerproof container and freeze for 5–6 hours.

3 Meanwhile, preheat the oven to 350°F/180°C and line a cookie sheet with parchment paper. Cut the pie dough into regular-size rectangles to accommodate a slice of the parfait. Place the pie dough rectangles on the sheet and top with another cookie sheet, which will keep the pie dough flat but crisp. Bake in the oven for 15 minutes, transfer to a wire rack, and let cool.

4 About 20 minutes before you are ready to serve, remove the parfait from the freezer. When it has softened, cut the parfait into slices and put each slice between 2 pieces of pie dough to make a "sandwich." Drizzle with the melted chocolate.

ONE ROLL FRUIT PIE

SERVES 8

INGREDIENTS
- 1⅛ CUPS ALL-PURPOSE FLOUR, PLUS EXTRA FOR DUSTING
- SCANT ½ CUP BUTTER, CUT INTO SMALL PIECES, PLUS EXTRA FOR GREASING
- 1 TBSP WATER
- 1 EGG, SEPARATED
- CRUSHED SUGAR CUBES, FOR SPRINKLING

FILLING
- 1 LB 5 OZ/600 G PREPARED FRUIT, SUCH AS RHUBARB, GOOSEBERRIES, OR PLUMS
- GENEROUS ⅓ CUP LIGHT BROWN SUGAR
- 1 TBSP GROUND GINGER

1 Place the flour in a large bowl, add the butter, and rub it in with your fingertips until the mixture resembles breadcrumbs. Add the water and mix together to form a soft dough. Cover and let chill in the refrigerator for 30 minutes.

2 Preheat the oven to 400°F/200°C. Grease a large cookie sheet. Roll out the dough on a lightly floured counter to a 14-inch/35-cm round. Transfer the round to the prepared cookie sheet and brush with the egg yolk.

3 To make the filling, mix the fruit with the sugar and ground ginger and pile it into the center of the pie dough. Turn in the edges of the dough all the way around. Brush the surface of the dough with the egg white and sprinkle with the crushed sugar cubes.

4 Bake in the preheated oven for 35 minutes, or until golden brown. Transfer to a serving plate and serve warm.

NEW YORK CHEESECAKE

SERVES 10

INGREDIENTS
- GENEROUS ½ CUP BUTTER
- 5½ OZ/150 G GRAHAM CRACKERS, FINELY CRUSHED
- 1 TBSP GRANULATED SUGAR
- 2 LB/900 G CREAM CHEESE
- 1¼ CUPS SUPERFINE SUGAR
- 2 TBSP ALL-PURPOSE FLOUR
- 1 TSP VANILLA EXTRACT
- FINELY GRATED ZEST OF 1 ORANGE
- FINELY GRATED ZEST OF 1 LEMON
- 3 EGGS
- 2 EGG YOLKS
- 1¼ CUPS HEAVY CREAM

1 Preheat the oven to 350°F/180°C. Place a small saucepan over low heat, add the butter, and heat until it melts, then remove from the heat, stir in the crushed crackers and granulated sugar, and mix through. Press the cracker mixture tightly into the bottom of a 9-inch/23-cm springform cake pan. Place in the oven and bake for 10 minutes. Remove from the oven and let cool on a wire rack.

2 Increase the oven temperature to 400°F/200°C. With an electric food mixer beat the cheese until creamy, then gradually add the superfine sugar and flour and beat until smooth. Increase the speed and beat in the vanilla extract, orange zest, and lemon zest, then beat in the eggs and egg yolks one at a time. Finally, beat in the cream. Scrape any excess from the sides and beaters of the mixer into the mixture. It should be light and whippy—beat on a faster setting if you need to.

3 Butter the sides of the cake pan and pour in the filling. Smooth the top, transfer to the preheated oven, and bake for 15 minutes, then reduce the temperature to 200°F/100°C and bake for an additional 30 minutes. Turn off the oven and let the cheesecake stand in it for 2 hours to cool and set. Cover and refrigerate overnight.

4 Slide a knife around the edge of the cake then unfasten the pan, cut the cheesecake into wedge-shaped slices, and serve.

STRAWBERRY
ECLAIRS

MAKES ABOUT 18

INGREDIENTS
PASTRY
- 4 TBSP UNSALTED BUTTER, PLUS EXTRA FOR GREASING
- ⅔ CUP WATER
- ½ CUP ALL-PURPOSE FLOUR
- 2 EGGS, BEATEN

- **FILLING**
- 1¾ CUPS STRAWBERRIES
- 2 TBSP CONFECTIONERS' SUGAR
- ⅔ CUP MASCARPONE CHEESE

1 Preheat the oven to 425°F/220°C. Grease 2 baking sheets. Heat the butter and water in a pan until boiling.

2 Remove from the heat, quickly tip in the flour, and beat until smooth.

3 Gradually beat in the eggs with an electric handheld mixer until glossy.

4 Spoon into a pastry bag with a large plain tip and pipe eighteen 3½-inch/9-cm strips on the baking sheets.

5 Bake for 15–20 minutes, until golden brown. Cut a slit down the side of each éclair to release steam. Bake for 2 minutes more. Cool on a wire rack.

6 Puree half the strawberries with the confectioners' sugar.

7 Finely chop the remaining strawberries and stir into the mascarpone.

8 Pipe or spoon the mascarpone mixture into the éclairs.

9 Serve the éclairs with the strawberry puree spooned over them.

5

BREAD & SAVORY

Baking bread by hand is enormously satisfying. The process involves taking flour, yeast, water, sugar, and salt and turning them into a delicious loaf of bread. The process may take some time, but the resulting crusty, warm, soft loaf is well worth it. This chapter also includes a delicious selection of savory options from pleasing pies to tempting tarts, plus a few mouthwatering muffins thrown in for good measure.

CRUSTY WHITE BREAD

MAKES 1 MEDIUM LOAF

INGREDIENTS
- 1 EGG
- 1 EGG YOLK
- ¾ –1 CUP LUKEWARM WATER
- 4½ CUPS WHITE BREAD FLOUR, PLUS EXTRA FOR DUSTING
- 1½ TSP SALT
- 2 TSP SUPERFINE SUGAR
- 1 TSP ACTIVE DRY YEAST
- 2 TBSP BUTTER, DICED
- VEGETABLE OIL, FOR BRUSHING

1 Lightly beat together the egg and egg yolk in a measuring cup. Stir in enough lukewarm water to make up to 1¼ cups.

2 Sift the flour and salt together into a bowl and stir in the sugar and yeast. Add the butter and rub it in with your fingertips until the mixture resembles breadcrumbs. Make a well in the center, pour in the egg mixture, and stir well with a wooden spoon until the dough begins to come together, then knead with your hands until it leaves the side of the bowl. Turn out onto a lightly floured counter and knead well for about 10 minutes, until smooth and elastic.

3 Brush a bowl with oil. Shape the dough into a ball, put it into the bowl, and put the bowl into a plastic bag or cover with a damp dish towel. Let rise in a warm place for 1–2 hours, until the dough has doubled in volume.

4 Brush a 7½ x 4½ x 3½-inch/ 19 x 12 x 9-cm loaf pan with oil. Turn out the dough onto a lightly floured counter, punch down with your fist, and knead for 1 minute. With lightly floured hands, shape the dough into a rectangle the same length as the pan and flatten slightly. Fold it lengthwise into 3 and place in the prepared pan, seam side down. Put the pan into a plastic bag or cover with a damp dish towel and let rise in a warm place for 30 minutes, until the dough has reached the top of the pan.

5 Preheat the oven to 425°F/220°C. Bake the loaf for 30 minutes, until it has shrunk from the sides of the pan, is golden brown, and sounds hollow when tapped on the bottom with your knuckles. Turn out onto a wire rack to cool.

MIXED SEED BREAD

MAKES 1 MEDIUM LOAF

INGREDIENTS
- 3¼ CUPS WHITE BREAD FLOUR, PLUS EXTRA FOR DUSTING
- SCANT 1¼ CUPS RYE FLOUR
- 1½ TSP SALT
- 1½ TBSP NONFAT DRY MILK
- 1 TBSP LIGHT BROWN SUGAR
- 1 TSP ACTIVE DRY YEAST
- 1½ TBSP SUNFLOWER OIL, PLUS EXTRA FOR BRUSHING
- 2 TSP LEMON JUICE
- 1¼ CUPS LUKEWARM WATER
- 1 TSP CARAWAY SEEDS
- ½ TSP POPPY SEEDS
- ½ TSP SESAME SEEDS

TOPPING
- 1 EGG WHITE
- 1 TBSP WATER
- 1 TBSP SUNFLOWER OR PUMPKIN SEEDS

1 Sift both types of flour and the salt together into a bowl and stir in the milk, sugar, and yeast. Make a well in the center and pour in the oil, lemon juice, and lukewarm water. Add the seeds. Stir well with a wooden spoon until the dough begins to come together, then knead with your hands until it leaves the side of the bowl. Turn out onto a lightly floured counter and knead well for about 10 minutes, until smooth and elastic.

2 Brush a bowl with oil. Shape the dough into a ball, put it into the bowl, and put the bowl into a plastic bag or cover with a damp dish towel. Let rise in a warm place for 1 hour, until the dough has doubled in volume.

3 Brush a 9 x 5 x 3-inch/23 x 13 x 8-cm loaf pan with oil. Turn out the dough onto a lightly floured counter, punch down with your fist, and knead for 1 minute. With lightly floured hands, shape the dough into a rectangle the same length as the pan and flatten slightly. Fold it lengthwise into 3 and place in the pan, seam side down. Put the pan into a plastic bag or cover with a damp dish towel and let rise in a warm place for 30 minutes, until the dough has reached the top of the pan.

4 Preheat the oven to 425°F/220°C. For the topping, lightly beat the egg white with the water in a bowl. Brush the top of the loaf with egg white glaze and sprinkle with the seeds. Bake for 30 minutes, until golden brown and the loaf sounds hollow when tapped on the bottom with your knuckles. Turn out onto a wire rack to cool.

WHOLE WHEAT
HARVEST BREAD

MAKES 1 SMALL LOAF

INGREDIENTS
- 2 CUPS WHOLE WHEAT BREAD FLOUR, PLUS EXTRA FOR DUSTING
- 1 TSP SALT
- 1 TBSP NONFAT DRY MILK
- 2 TBSP SOFT BROWN SUGAR
- 1 TSP ACTIVE DRY YEAST
- 1½ TBSP VEGETABLE OIL, PLUS EXTRA FOR BRUSHING
- ¾ CUP LUKEWARM WATER

1 Sift the flour and salt together into a bowl, tip in the bran from the sifter, and stir in the milk, sugar, and yeast. Make a well in the center and pour in the oil and lukewarm water. Stir well with a wooden spoon until the dough begins to come together, then knead with your hands until it leaves the side of the bowl. Turn out onto a lightly floured counter and knead well for about 10 minutes, until smooth and elastic.

2 Brush a bowl with oil. Shape the dough into a ball, put it into the bowl, and put the bowl into a plastic bag or cover with a damp dish towel. Let rise in a warm place for 1 hour, until the dough has doubled in volume.

3 Brush a 6½ x 4¼ x 3¼-inch/17 x 11 x 8-cm loaf pan with oil. Turn out the dough onto a lightly floured counter, punch down with your fist, and knead for 1 minute. With lightly floured hands, shape the dough into a rectangle the same length as the pan and flatten slightly. Fold it lengthwise into 3 and place in the prepared pan, seam side down. Put the pan into a plastic bag or cover with a damp dish towel and let rise in a warm place for 30 minutes, until the dough has reached the top of the pan.

4 Preheat the oven to 425°F/220°C. Bake the loaf for about 30 minutes, until it has shrunk from the sides of the pan, the crust is golden brown, and it sounds hollow when tapped on the bottom with your knuckles. Turn out onto a wire rack to cool.

TOMATO & ROSEMARY
FOCACCIA

MAKES 1 LOAF

INGREDIENTS
- 4½ CUPS WHITE BREAD FLOUR, PLUS EXTRA FOR DUSTING
- 1½ TSP SALT
- 1½ TSP ACTIVE DRY YEAST
- 2 TBSP CHOPPED FRESH ROSEMARY, PLUS EXTRA SPRIGS TO GARNISH
- 6 TBSP EXTRA VIRGIN OLIVE OIL, PLUS EXTRA FOR BRUSHING
- 1¼ CUPS LUKEWARM WATER
- 6 SUN-DRIED TOMATOES IN OIL, DRAINED
- 1 TSP COARSE SEA SALT

1 Sift the flour and salt together into a bowl and stir in the yeast and rosemary. Make a well in the center, pour in 4 tablespoons of the oil, and mix quickly with a wooden spoon. Gradually stir in the lukewarm water but do not overmix. Turn out onto a lightly floured counter and knead for 2 minutes. The dough will be quite wet; do not add more flour.

2 Brush a bowl with oil. Shape the dough into a ball, put it into the bowl, and cover with a damp dish towel. Let rise in a warm place for 2 hours, until doubled in volume.

3 Brush a cookie sheet with oil. Turn out the dough onto a lightly floured counter and punch down with your fist, then knead for 1 minute. Put the dough onto the prepared cookie sheet and press out into an even layer. Cover the cookie sheet with a damp dish towel and let rise in a warm place for 1 hour.

4 Preheat the oven to 475°F/240°C. Cut the sun-dried tomatoes into pieces. Whisk the remaining oil with a little water in a bowl. Dip your fingers into the oil mixture and press them into the dough to make dimples all over the loaf. Sprinkle with the sea salt. Press the tomato pieces into some of the dimples, drizzle with the remaining oil mixture, and sprinkle the loaf with the rosemary sprigs.

5 Reduce the oven temperature to 425°F/220°C and bake the focaccia for 20 minutes, until golden brown. Transfer to a wire rack to cool slightly, then serve while still warm.

BAGELS

MAKES 10

INGREDIENTS
- 3 CUPS WHITE BREAD FLOUR, PLUS EXTRA FOR DUSTING
- 2 TSP SALT
- 1 ENVELOPE ACTIVE DRY YEAST
- 1 TBSP LIGHTLY BEATEN EGG
- SCANT 1 CUP LUKEWARM WATER
- VEGETABLE OIL, FOR BRUSHING
- 1 EGG WHITE
- 2 TBSP WATER
- 2 TBSP CARAWAY SEEDS

1 Sift the flour and salt together into a bowl and stir in the yeast. Make a well in the center, pour in the egg and lukewarm water, and mix to a dough. Turn out onto a lightly floured counter and knead well for about 10 minutes, until smooth.

2 Brush a bowl with oil. Shape the dough into a ball, place it in the bowl, and put the bowl into a plastic bag or cover with a damp dish towel. Let rise in a warm place for 1 hour, until the dough has doubled in volume.

3 Brush 2 cookie sheets with oil and dust a baking sheet with flour. Turn out the dough onto a lightly floured counter and punch down with your fist. Knead for 2 minutes, then divide into 10 pieces. Shape each piece into a ball and let rest for 5 minutes. Gently flatten each ball with a lightly floured hand and make a hole in the center with the handle of a wooden spoon. Put the bagels on the floured sheet, put it into a plastic bag or cover with a damp dish towel, and let rise in a warm place for 20 minutes.

4 Meanwhile, preheat the oven to 425°F/220°C and bring a large pan of water to a boil. Reduce the heat until the water is barely simmering, then add 2 bagels. Poach for 1 minute, then turn over, and poach for 30 seconds more. Remove with a slotted spoon and drain on a dish towel. Poach the remaining bagels in the same way.

5 Transfer the bagels to the oiled cookie sheets. Beat the egg white with 2 teaspoons of the water in a bowl and brush it over the bagels. Sprinkle with the caraway seeds and bake for 25–30 minutes, until golden brown. Transfer to a wire rack to cool.

IRISH SODA
BREAD

MAKES 1 LOAF

INGREDIENTS
- VEGETABLE OIL, FOR BRUSHING
- 4 CUPS ALL-PURPOSE FLOUR,
  PLUS EXTRA FOR DUSTING
- 1 TSP SALT
- 1 TSP BAKING SODA
- 1¾ CUPS BUTTERMILK

1 Preheat the oven to 425°F/220°C. Brush a cookie sheet with oil.

2 Sift the flour, salt, and baking soda together into a bowl. Make a well in the center and pour in most of the buttermilk. Mix well, first with a wooden spoon and then with your hands. The dough should be very soft but not too wet. If necessary, add the remaining buttermilk.

3 Turn out the dough onto a lightly floured counter and knead lightly and briefly. Shape into an 8-inch/20-cm round. Put the loaf onto the prepared cookie sheet and cut a cross in the top with a sharp knife.

4 Bake for 25–30 minutes, until golden brown and the loaf sounds hollow when tapped on the bottom with your knuckles. Transfer to a wire rack to cool slightly and serve warm.

FLAT BREAD WITH ONION & ROSEMARY

MAKES 1 LOAF

INGREDIENTS
- 4 CUPS WHITE BREAD FLOUR, PLUS EXTRA FOR DUSTING
- ½ TSP SALT
- 1½ TSP ACTIVE DRY YEAST
- 2 TBSP CHOPPED FRESH ROSEMARY, PLUS SMALL SPRIGS TO GARNISH
- 5 TBSP EXTRA VIRGIN OLIVE OIL, PLUS EXTRA FOR BRUSHING
- 1¼ CUPS LUKEWARM WATER
- 1 RED ONION, THINLY SLICED AND PUSHED OUT INTO RINGS
- 1 TBSP COARSE SEA SALT

1 Sift the flour and salt together into a bowl and stir in the yeast and rosemary. Make a well in the center and pour in 3 tablespoons of the oil and all of the lukewarm water. Stir well with a wooden spoon until the dough begins to come together, then knead with your hands until it leaves the side of the bowl. Turn out onto a lightly floured counter and knead well for about 10 minutes, until smooth and elastic.

2 Brush a bowl with oil. Shape the dough into a ball, put it into the bowl, and put the bowl into a plastic bag or cover with a damp dish towel. Let rise in a warm place for 1 hour, until the dough has doubled in volume.

3 Brush a cookie sheet with oil. Turn out the dough onto a lightly floured counter, punch down with your fist, and knead for 1 minute. Roll out the dough to a round about 12 inches/30 cm in diameter and put it on the prepared cookie sheet. Put the cookie sheet into a plastic bag or cover with a damp dish towel and let rise in a warm place for 20–30 minutes.

4 Preheat the oven to 400°F/200°C. Using the handle of a wooden spoon, make indentations all over the surface of the loaf. Spread the onion rings over the top, drizzle with the remaining oil, and sprinkle with the sea salt. Bake for 20 minutes. Sprinkle with the rosemary sprigs, return to the oven, and bake for 5 minutes more, until golden brown. Transfer to a wire rack to cool slightly and serve warm.

CHEESE & CHIVE BREAD

SERVES 8

INGREDIENTS
- BUTTER, FOR GREASING
- GENEROUS 1½ CUPS SELF-RISING FLOUR
- 1 TSP SALT
- 1 TSP MUSTARD POWDER
- 1 CUP GRATED SHARP CHEESE
- 2 TBSP CHOPPED FRESH CHIVES
- 1 EGG, LIGHTLY BEATEN
- 2 TBSP BUTTER, MELTED
- ⅔ CUP MILK

1 Grease a 9-inch/23-cm square cake pan with butter and line the bottom with parchment paper.

2 Sift the self-rising flour, salt, and mustard powder together into a large mixing bowl.

3 Reserve 3 tablespoons of the grated sharp cheese for sprinkling over the top of the loaf before baking in the oven.

4 Stir the remaining cheese into the bowl along with the chopped fresh chives. Mix well together.

5 Add the beaten egg, melted butter, and milk and stir the mixture thoroughly to combine.

6 Pour the mixture into the prepared pan and spread out evenly with a knife or spatula. Sprinkle over the reserved grated cheese.

7 Bake in a preheated oven, 375°F/190°C, for about 30 minutes.

8 Let the bread cool slightly in the pan, then turn out onto a wire rack to cool completely. Cut into triangles to serve.

OLIVE & SUN-DRIED TOMATO BREAD

MAKES 2 LOAVES

INGREDIENTS
- 3½ CUPS ALL-PURPOSE FLOUR, PLUS EXTRA FOR DUSTING
- 1 TSP SALT
- 1 ENVELOPE ACTIVE DRY YEAST
- 1 TSP BROWN SUGAR
- 1 TBSP CHOPPED FRESH THYME
- SCANT 1 CUP LUKEWARM WATER
- 4 TBSP OLIVE OIL, PLUS EXTRA FOR BRUSHING
- ½ CUP BLACK OLIVES, PITTED AND SLICED
- ½ CUP GREEN OLIVES, PITTED AND SLICED
- 1¾ CUPS DRAINED SUN-DRIED TOMATOES IN OIL, SLICED
- 1 EGG YOLK, BEATEN

1 Sift the flour and salt together into a bowl and stir in the yeast, sugar, and thyme. Make a well in the center and pour in the lukewarm water and oil. Stir well with a wooden spoon until the dough begins to come together, then knead with your hands until it leaves the side of the bowl. Turn out onto a lightly floured counter and knead in the olives and sun-dried tomatoes, then knead for 5 minutes more, until the dough is smooth and elastic.

2 Brush a bowl with oil. Shape the dough into a ball, put it into the bowl, and put the bowl into a plastic bag or cover with a damp dish towel. Let rise in a warm place for 1–1½ hours, until the dough has doubled in volume.

3 Dust a cookie sheet with flour. Turn out the dough onto a lightly floured counter and punch down with your fist. Cut it in half and with lightly floured hands, shape each half into a round or oval. Put them on the prepared cookie sheet and put the cookie sheet into a plastic bag or cover with a damp dish towel. Let rise in a warm place for 45 minutes.

4 Preheat the oven to 400°F/200°C. Make 3 shallow diagonal slashes on the top of each loaf and brush with the beaten egg yolk. Bake for 40 minutes, until golden brown and the loaves sound hollow when tapped on the bottom with your knuckles. Transfer to a wire rack to cool.

BRIOCHE BRAID

MAKES 1 LOAF

INGREDIENTS
- 2½ CUPS WHITE BREAD FLOUR
- ½ TSP SALT
- ½ CUP UNSALTED BUTTER, CHILLED AND DICED
- 2 TBSP SUPERFINE SUGAR
- 1 ENVELOPE ACTIVE DRY YEAST
- 2 EGGS, BEATEN
- GENEROUS ¼ CUP WARM MILK
- BEATEN EGG, TO GLAZE

1 Sift the flour and salt into a large mixing bowl. Add the butter and rub into the flour with your fingertips. Stir in the sugar and yeast. Make a well in the center.

2 Pour the eggs and milk into the bowl. Stir well to make a soft dough. Turn the dough onto a lightly floured surface and knead for 5–10 minutes, until the dough is smooth and elastic, sprinkling with a little more flour if the dough becomes sticky.

3 Grease a large baking sheet. Divide the dough into 3 equal pieces and shape each into a rope about 14 inches/ 35 cm long. Place the ropes side by side and press them together at one end. Braid the ropes, then pinch the ends together.

4 Transfer the braid to the baking sheet, cover loosely with oiled plastic wrap, and let stand in a warm place for about 1 hour, until almost doubled in size.

5 Preheat the oven to 375°F/190°C. Brush the braid with the beaten egg. Bake in the preheated oven for 30–35 minutes, until risen and golden brown, covering loosely with foil after 25 minutes to prevent from become too brown. Serve warm.

PARMESAN & PINE NUT
MUFFINS

MAKES 12

INGREDIENTS
- OIL OR MELTED BUTTER, FOR GREASING (IF USING)
- 2 CUPS ALL-PURPOSE FLOUR
- 1 TBSP BAKING POWDER
- ⅛ TSP SALT
- ¾ CUP FRESHLY GRATED PARMESAN CHEESE
- ½ CUP PINE NUTS
- 2 LARGE EGGS
- 1 CUP BUTTERMILK
- 6 TBSP SUNFLOWER OIL OR MELTED, COOLED BUTTER
- PEPPER

TOPPING
- 4 TSP FRESHLY GRATED PARMESAN CHEESE
- ¼ CUP PINE NUTS

1 Preheat the oven to 400°F/200°C. Grease a 12-cup muffin pan or line with 12 muffin paper liners.

2 To make the topping, mix together the Parmesan cheese and pine nuts and set aside.

3 To make the muffins, sift together the flour, baking powder, salt, and pepper to taste into a large bowl. Stir in the Parmesan cheese and pine nuts.

4 Lightly beat the eggs in a large pitcher or bowl, then beat in the buttermilk and oil. Make a well in the center of the dry ingredients and pour in the beaten liquid ingredients. Stir gently until just combined; do not overmix.

5 Spoon the batter into the prepared muffin pan. Scatter the topping over the muffins. Bake in the preheated oven for about 20 minutes, until well risen, golden brown, and firm to the touch.

6 Let the muffins cool in the pan for 5 minutes, then serve warm.

CHILE CORNBREAD
MUFFINS

MAKES 12

INGREDIENTS
- 1¼ CUPS ALL-PURPOSE FLOUR
- 4 TSP BAKING POWDER
- 1¼ CUPS CORNMEAL
- 2 TBSP SUPERFINE SUGAR
- 1 TSP SALT
- 4 SCALLIONS, TRIMMED AND FINELY CHOPPED
- 1 RED CHILE PEPPER, SEEDED AND FINELY CHOPPED
- 3 EGGS, BEATEN
- ⅔ CUP PLAIN YOGURT
- ⅔ CUP MILK

1 Preheat the oven to 400°F/200°C. Put 12 paper muffin liners in a 12-hole muffin pan.

2 Sift the flour and baking powder into a large bowl. Stir in the cornmeal, sugar, salt, scallions, and chile pepper. Beat together the eggs, yogurt, and milk, then pour into the flour mixture and beat until just combined. Spoon the mixture into the muffin liners.

3 Bake the muffins in the preheated oven for 15–20 minutes, until risen, golden, and just firm to the touch. Serve warm.

SMOKED SALMON, DILL & HORSERADISH TARTLETS

MAKES 6

INGREDIENTS
PIE DOUGH
- HEAPING ¾ CUP ALL-PURPOSE FLOUR, PLUS EXTRA FOR DUSTING
- PINCH OF SALT
- 5 TBSP COLD BUTTER, CUT INTO PIECES, PLUS EXTRA FOR GREASING
- COLD WATER

FILLING
- ½ CUP SOUR CREAM
- 1 TSP CREAMED HORSERADISH
- ½ TSP LEMON JUICE
- 1 TSP SPANISH CAPERS, CHOPPED
- 3 EGG YOLKS
- 7 OZ/200 G SMOKED SALMON TRIMMINGS
- BUNCH FRESH DILL, CHOPPED, PLUS EXTRA SPRIGS TO GARNISH
- SALT AND PEPPER

1 Grease six fluted 3½-inch/9-cm loose-bottom tartlet pans. Sift the flour and salt into a food processor, add the butter, and process until the mixture resembles fine breadcrumbs. Transfer the mixture to a large bowl and add a little cold water, just enough to bring the dough together.

2 Turn out onto a floured counter and divide into 6 equal-size pieces. Roll each piece to fit the tartlet pans. Carefully fit each piece of dough in its shell and press well to fit the pan. Roll the rolling pin over the pan to neaten the edges and trim the excess dough.

3 Cut 6 pieces of parchment paper and fit a piece into each tartlet, fill with dried beans, and let chill in the refrigerator for 30 minutes. Meanwhile, preheat the oven to 400°F/200°C.

4 Bake the tartlet shells blind for 10 minutes in the preheated oven, then remove the beans and parchment paper.

5 Meanwhile, put the sour cream, horseradish, lemon juice, capers, and salt and pepper into a bowl and mix well. Add the egg yolks, the smoked salmon, and the dill and carefully mix again.

6 Divide the filling among the tartlet shells and return to the oven for 10 minutes. Let cool in the pans for 5 minutes before serving garnished with dill sprigs.

BLEU CHEESE & WALNUT TARTLETS

MAKES 12

INGREDIENTS
PIE DOUGH
- 1½ CUPS ALL-PURPOSE FLOUR, PLUS EXTRA FOR DUSTING
- PINCH OF CELERY SALT
- 5 TBSP COLD BUTTER, CUT INTO PIECES, PLUS EXTRA FOR GREASING
- ¼ CUP WALNUT HALVES, CHOPPED IN A FOOD PROCESSOR
- COLD WATER

FILLING
- 2 TBSP BUTTER
- 2 CELERY STALKS, TRIMMED AND FINELY CHOPPED
- 1 SMALL LEEK, TRIMMED AND FINELY CHOPPED
- SCANT 1 CUP HEAVY CREAM, PLUS 2 TBSP EXTRA
- 7 OZ/200 G BLEU CHEESE
- 3 EGG YOLKS
- SALT AND PEPPER

1 Lightly grease a 12-hole muffin pan with 3-inch/7.5-cm cups. Sift the flour and celery salt into a food processor, add the butter, and process until the mixture resembles fine breadcrumbs. Transfer the mixture to a bowl and add the walnuts and a little cold water, just enough to bring the dough together.

2 Turn out onto a floured counter and cut the dough in half. Roll out the first piece and cut out six 3½-inch/9-cm circles. Take each circle and roll out to 4½ inches/12 cm diameter and fit into the muffin holes, pressing to fill the holes. Do the same with the remaining dough. Put a piece of parchment paper in each hole, fill with dried beans, then put the pan in the refrigerator to chill for 30 minutes. Meanwhile, preheat the oven to 400°F/200°C.

3 Remove the muffin pan from the refrigerator and bake blind the tartlets for 10 minutes in the preheated oven, then carefully remove the paper and beans.

4 For the filling, melt the butter in a skillet, add the celery and leek, and cook for 15 minutes, until soft. Add 2 tablespoons of the heavy cream and crumble in the bleu cheese, mix well, an d season with salt and pepper. Bring the remaining cream to a simmer in another pan, then pour onto the egg yolks, stirring all the time. Mix in the bleu cheese mixture and spoon into the pastry shells. Bake for 10 minutes, then turn the pan around in the oven and bake for an additional 5 minutes. Let cool in the pan for 5 minutes before serving.

ASPARAGUS & CHEESE TART

SERVES 6

INGREDIENTS
- FLOUR FOR DUSTING
- 9 OZ/250 G PREPARED FLAKY PASTRY, THAWED IF FROZEN
- 9 OZ/250 G ASPARAGUS
- 1 TBSP VEGETABLE OIL
- 1 RED ONION, FINELY CHOPPED
- 2 TBSP CHOPPED HAZELNUTS
- 7 OZ/200 G GOAT CHEESE
- 2 EGGS, BEATEN
- 4 TBSP LIGHT CREAM
- SALT AND PEPPER

1 On a lightly floured counter, roll out the pie dough and line a 9½-inch/24-cm loose-bottom tart pan. Prick the bottom of the tart shell with a fork and chill in the refrigerator for 30 minutes. Meanwhile, preheat the oven to 375°F/190°C.

2 Line the tart shell with parchment paper and dried beans and bake blind in a preheated oven for about 15 minutes.

3 Remove the paper and beans and bake for another 15 minutes.

4 Cook the asparagus in boiling water for 2–3 minutes, drain, and cut into bite-size pieces.

5 Heat the oil in a small skillet. Add the onion and cook over low heat, stirring occasionally for about 5 minutes, until soft and lightly golden. Spoon the asparagus, onion, and hazelnuts into the prepared tart shell, spreading them out evenly.

6 Beat together the cheese, eggs, and cream until smooth, or process in a blender until smooth. Season well with salt and pepper, then pour the mixture over the asparagus, onion, and hazelnuts.

7 Bake the tart for 15–20 minutes, or until the cheese filling is just set. Serve warm or cold.

BACON, ONION & PARMESAN TART

SERVES 6

INGREDIENTS
- 9 OZ/250 G FRESH PREPARED UNSWEETENED PASTRY
- 8 TSP BUTTER
- 2¾ OZ/75 G BACON, CHOPPED
- 1LB 9 OZ/700 G ONIONS, PEELED AND THINLY SLICED
- 2 EGGS, BEATEN
- SCANT ½ CUP GRATED PARMESAN CHEESE
- 1 TSP DRIED SAGE
- SALT AND PEPPER

1 Roll out the pastry on a lightly floured counter and line a 9½-inch/24-cm loose-bottom tart pan.

2 Prick the bottom of the pastry with a fork and let chill for 30 minutes.

3 Heat the butter in a pan, add the chopped bacon and sliced onions, and sweat them over a low heat for about 25 minutes, or until tender. If the onion slices start to brown, add 1 tbsp water to the pan. Meanwhile, preheat the oven to 350°F/180°C.

4 Add the beaten eggs to the onion mixture and stir in the cheese, sage, and salt and pepper to taste.

5 Spoon the filling into the prepared pie shell.

6 Bake in the preheated oven for 20–30 minutes, or until the tart has just set.

7 Let cool slightly in the pan, then serve the tart warm or cold.

POTATO & RED ONION PIE

SERVES 6

INGREDIENTS
- BUTTER, FOR GREASING
- 1 LB 9 OZ/700 G POTATOES, PEELED AND THINLY SLICED
- 2 SCALLIONS, FINELY CHOPPED
- 1 RED ONION, FINELY CHOPPED
- ⅔ CUP HEAVY CREAM
- 1 LB FRESH PREPARED PUFF PASTRY
- 2 EGGS, BEATEN
- SALT AND PEPPER

1 Preheat the oven to 400°F/200°C. Lightly grease a cookie sheet. Bring a pan of water to a boil, then add the sliced potatoes. Bring back to a boil and simmer for a few minutes. Drain the potato slices and let cool. Dry off any excess moisture with paper towels.

2 In a bowl, mix together the scallions, red onion, and the cooled potato slices. Stir in 2 tbsp of the cream and plenty of salt and pepper.

3 Divide the pastry in half and roll out one piece to a 9-inch/23-cm circle. Roll the remaining pastry to a 10-inch/25-cm circle.

4 Place the smaller circle onto the cookie sheet and top with the potato mixture, leaving a 1-inch/2.5-cm border. Brush this border with a little of the beaten egg.

5 Top with the larger circle of pastry, seal well, and crimp the edges of the pastry. Cut a steam vent in the middle of the pastry and mark with a pattern. Brush with the beaten egg and bake in a preheated oven for 30 minutes.

6 Mix the remaining beaten egg with the rest of the cream and pour into the pie through the steam vent. Return to the oven for 15 minutes, then let cool for 30 minutes. Serve warm or cold.